Entrepreneurial Giants

Drawing Strength from Biblical Principles for Business Breakthroughs

A lifeline for those navigating the deep, uncharted waters of entrepreneurship.

By

Dr. Roy L. Johnson, Jr.

Entrepreneurial Giants by Dr. Roy L. Johnson, Jr.

Copyright © 2023

Foreword Written By:

Sonja R. Lowe, Ph.D.

Proofreading and Editing:

Dr. Amanda (@mrs_perfect99)

Acknowledgments

To My Heavenly Father and the Holy Spirit...

I must say this has been such AN AMAZING JOURNEY! My heart is full, and I am in awe at the wonderous works crafted and entrusted through me to reach, teach, educate, empower, and inspire your nation of people I have been called to serve!

However, I would be remiss if I didn't start by expressing my deepest gratitude to the Divine Architect of all things, the Creator of every dream and vision, and the Guiding Light through the journey of life, God.

To the Holy Spirit, the silent whisperer of wisdom, the source of inspiration, and the gentle force that ignites our spirits, I owe an immeasurable debt of gratitude.

In writing "Entrepreneurial Giants: Drawing Strength from Biblical Principles for Business Breakthroughs," I am acutely aware that this book is not solely the product of my effort but a testament to the divine vision bestowed upon me. It is a reminder that we are instruments in a grand symphony, and the true Composer is above.

Thank you, Almighty, for your continuous guidance and for ordering my steps, often where I couldn't see, but where I needed to be. Thank you for the courage to embark on this profound assignment and the obedience to carry it through in this season of life.

As I pen these words of acknowledgment, I am reminded that every word, every idea, and every page is a result of Your divine orchestration. This book is a labor of love, and I dedicate it to You, for without Your wisdom, grace, and unwavering presence, it would remain but a dream.

May "Entrepreneurial Giants: Drawing Strength from Biblical Principles for Business Breakthroughs" serve as a beacon of hope and a source of empowerment to aspiring entrepreneurs and those journeying through the maze of entrepreneurship. May it shine Your light upon their paths, guiding them to greatness, resilience, and success.

In Humble Reverence and Heartfelt Gratitude,

Roy L. Johnson, Jr., Ph.D.

To my dearest parents, Roy Johnson, Sr. and Lola Johnson...

Where do I begin to express the depth of my gratitude for your unwavering support and unconditional love? You have been my pillars of strength, my guiding stars, and my greatest cheerleaders throughout every chapter of my life.

Your support, both knowingly and unknowingly, has been the wind beneath my wings, propelling me forward in times of doubt and uncertainty. Your love has been a constant source of inspiration, reminding me that with your belief in me, I can achieve the impossible.

With every stroke of the keyboard, I am fanatically reminded of the countless sacrifices you've made, the late nights you've stayed up with me, and the endless encouragement you've provided. Your belief in my dreams has been a driving force, pushing me to reach for the stars.

This book, "Entrepreneurial Giants: Drawing Strength from Biblical Principles for Business Breakthroughs," stands as a testament to your unwavering faith in me. It's a reflection of the values, resilience, and determination you instilled in me from a young age. Your love has not only shaped me as an individual but has also guided me on this incredible journey of entrepreneurship.

Thank you, Mom and Dad, for being my rock, my compass, and my biggest supporters. Your love is the fuel that keeps me going, and your presence in my life is a gift beyond measure.

With All My Love and Gratitude,

Roy L. Johnson, Jr., Ph.D.

To my beloved siblings, Rodney, LoShaundra, and LoShanah...

There are few treasures as precious as family, and in my case, you three are the brightest gems in my constellation. Your unwavering support, boundless love, and the laughter we've shared are cherished gifts that have enriched my life beyond measure.

Through the ups and downs, twists, and turns, you've stood by my side with unfaltering support. Your belief in my dreams, even when they seemed audacious, has been a source of immeasurable strength. Your encouragement has been a constant reminder that I am never alone on this path of entrepreneurship.

But beyond the support, it's the moments of laughter, the heartwarming calls just to say, "I love you," and the countless shared memories that have painted the canvas of my life with vibrant colors. In those moments, I've found solace, joy, and the reassurance that family is a bond that can weather any storm.

This book, "Entrepreneurial Giants: Drawing Strength from Biblical Principles for Business Breakthroughs," is not just a reflection of my journey but a tribute to the values, love, and resilience you have all instilled and cultivated in me as your big brother. It's a testament to the profound impact you've had on my life, as individuals who truly believe in the power of family.

As I write these words of acknowledgment, I want to express my deepest gratitude for being not just siblings but my pillars of strength, my confidants, and my greatest friends. Your love has illuminated the path of my life, and I carry your unwavering support with me on this incredible journey.

Thank you, Rodney, LoShaundra, and LoShanah, for being my constants in a world of change. Your love is the melody that brightens my days, and your presence in my life is a treasure beyond measure.

With All My Love and Gratitude,

Your Big Brother,

Roy L. Johnson, Jr., Ph.D.

To my dearest friend and unwavering supporter, David Price...

In the tapestry of life, friendships are the threads that add color, texture, and depth to our journey. You, my dear friend, are not just a thread but a vibrant tapestry of support, loyalty, and unwavering encouragement.

Throughout the years, you have stood by my side, not just as a friend but as a pillar of strength. Your unwavering support has been a beacon of light in my darkest hours and a source of boundless joy in moments of triumph. You've celebrated my successes and uplifted me in times of doubt.

Your belief in me and my endeavors has been a driving force, pushing me to reach for the stars. Your friendship has been a constant reminder that, in this vast world, there is someone who always has my back.

As I pen these words, I want to express my deepest gratitude for your friendship, for being the one I can turn to in times of need and in moments of celebration. Your unwavering support for my entrepreneurial journey has been a precious gift that I hold close to my heart.

"Entrepreneurial Giants: Drawing Strength from Biblical Principles for Business Breakthroughs," is an incomparable testament not just to my journey but to the incredible people like you who have navigated these uncharted waters with me. It's a tribute to the bonds of friendship and the profound impact they can have on our lives.

David, your friendship is a treasure beyond measure, and I want to thank you from the bottom of my heart for always being there, for believing in me, and for supporting me in every endeavor.

With Heartfelt Gratitude and the Warmest of Wishes,

Roy L. Johnson, Jr., Ph.D.

To my dearest friend, Quincy "QTH" Hale...

Over the past 20 years, our friendship has been a beacon of unwavering support, trust, and laughter. It's not every day that one finds a confidant and a true supporter like you, and for that, I am immensely grateful.

From our early days at Texas Children's Hospital to the countless moments we've shared since, you've been a constant source of encouragement, motivation, and lightheartedness. Your ability to find humor in every situation, no matter how challenging, has often been the ray of sunshine on my cloudiest days.

You've shown an extraordinary willingness to lend a listening ear, to have my back in both the good times and the tough times, and to uplift and inspire with your words and actions. Your unwavering support and your knack for bringing smiles and laughter to my life are qualities I deeply cherish.

In this ever-changing journey of life, it's the steadfast and genuine friendships like ours that make the voyage not only bearable but truly wonderful. So, Quincy, I want to take a moment to extend my heartfelt gratitude. Thank you for being my confidant, my supporter, and my friend for these remarkable two decades. I look forward to the many more years of laughter and shared memories to come.

With sincere appreciation and the warmest regards,

Your Genuine Friend and Brother,

Roy L. Johnson, Jr., Ph.D.

To my lifelong friend, confidant, and unwavering supporter, Arthur "Coach A.P." Patton...

Over the course of more than three decades, our friendship has been a treasure beyond measure. You are, without a doubt, one of the most remarkable people I've had the privilege of knowing since our elementary school days, and your steadfast friendship has been a constant source of strength and solace.

Through the years, I've come to recognize you not only as a true friend but as a genuine gem in the lives of those fortunate enough to know you. Your ability to go out of your way for the people you care about, to lend a listening ear when needed most, and to have their backs, including mine, in times of challenge, is nothing short of extraordinary.

But your support transcends mere actions; it's the profound encouragement, unwavering uplifting, and motivating spirit that you bring to our friendship that sets you apart. You have an uncanny knack for finding humor and positivity in even the most challenging moments, effortlessly placing a smile upon my face when I needed it most.

Arthur, "Coach A.P.," you possess a rare gift – the ability to make sense of things when I can't see or think clearly. In your company, I've discovered clarity, comfort, and an unmatched sense of camaraderie.

In life, it's the extraordinary friendships like ours that make each day brighter and every challenge surmountable. So, from the depths of my heart, I want to express my deepest gratitude for being the incredible friend that you are. Your presence in my life is a treasure I hold dear, and I look forward to the many more years of shared laughter and cherished moments.

With the utmost appreciation and boundless respect,

Your Best Friend and Loving Brother,

Roy L. Johnson, Jr., Ph.D.

To the exceptional Dr. Sonja Lowe...

There are leaders and visionaries who not only inspire but also nurture the dreams of others. You, Dr. Lowe, are the embodiment of such leadership—visionary, unwavering in faith, and a guiding light for countless aspiring souls, including me.

Your belief in my potential, even when I couldn't see it within myself, has been a source of profound inspiration. When you uttered those transformative words, "You need a book of your own," it was as if you breathed life into a dream, I didn't dare dream. Your unwavering encouragement, your uplifting words, and your motivating presence have been the cornerstones of this journey.

But your mentorship transcends the boundaries of this book. You've shown me the art of looking at the bigger picture, envisioning greatness when it seems beyond reach.

Your unwavering faith has not only given birth to "Entrepreneurial Giants: Drawing Strength from Biblical Principles for Business Breakthroughs," but has also ignited a fire within me to believe in the limitless possibilities of life.

As I mediate and utter these words of acknowledgment, I am overwhelmingly grateful for your leadership, your faith in my potential, and your ability to see the extraordinary in the ordinary. This book is a tribute to your mentorship, your vision, and the incredible impact you've had on my life's journey.

Dr. Lowe, you are not just a leader; you are a beacon of inspiration, a testament to the power of unwavering faith, and a guiding star for all who aspire to achieve greatness. As you always express, "Embrace Your Greatness."

Thank you for believing in me and thank you for showing me that the path to success begins with a visionary leader.

With Deepest Gratitude and the Warmest of Wishes,

Roy L. Johnson, Jr., Ph.D.

Foreword

Who is an Entrepreneur? An entrepreneur is an individual who takes the practical and intellectual initiative to create, develop, organize, and manage a business, typically with the goal of generating profit or achieving a specific purpose. Entrepreneurs are characterized by their astute willingness to take calculated risks, innovate, and invest their resources, including time, capital, and effort, into new or existing ventures. They are often driven by a vision, a passion for solving problems, and a desire to seize opportunities in the marketplace. Entrepreneurs play an evident critical role in driving economic growth and innovation by introducing new products, services, processes, or business models that can disrupt industries and create value for themselves and society as a whole.

But... there are many obstacles and setbacks that may arise on the journey. A firm foundation is mandatory for strength and success. As a marketplace entrepreneur, biblical principles are the dependable building blocks to building strength as you build and create an impactful and successful business.

As the founder and President of 1 Embrace Inc. Ministries, Strategic Growth Leaders Business & Bible University (SGLU) and BARE The Experience, I have been blessed to work with and coach entrepreneurs and leaders in the marketplace while using biblical principles. I remember a time I was attacked in the marketplace for my unwavering decision not to compromise biblical principles. I was committed to honoring God no matter what. The flesh wanted to react differently than the principles instilled, but I knew my business breakthrough was attached to my discipline and obedience. I quickly learned and coined my own personal quote, "We all have greatness within us; we must embrace it and let the world see it!"

Standing up in the marketplace to become an entrepreneurial giant and drawing strength from biblical principles for business breakthroughs is an act of profound significance. It means embracing a path of unwavering determination, resilience, and ethical integrity in the business world.

By grounding our entrepreneurial journey in timeless biblical wisdom, we not only find divine guidance for making sound decisions and fostering unity but also tap into a wellspring of faith that propels us beyond the limits of our comfort zones.

It reminds us that our pursuit of success is not just about personal gain but also about making a positive impact on the world. When we stand up with these supernatural principles as our foundation, we become not just business leaders but also champions of integrity, empathy, and lasting transformation.

Get ready to be inspired, motivated, and equipped with the tools and wisdom to not only succeed in your entrepreneurial journey but to do so while leaving a lasting legacy of positive change in your wake. Dr. Roy Johnson, Jr. has a profound story of how these principles helped him; his story is just the beginning of many more. Within these pages, you will find the keys to unlocking your unique potential as an entrepreneurial giant.

As we delve into "Entrepreneurial Giants, Drawing Strength from Biblical Principles for Business Breakthroughs, we invite you to join us in exploring the fusion of biblical principles and modern entrepreneurship. Dr. Roy Johnson Jr.'s remarkable journey and unwavering commitment to educating individuals to use their God-given gifts will serve as an inspiring backdrop against which we will uncover the profound lessons and insights that can guide us all toward unprecedented business breakthroughs.

In this extraordinary book, Dr. Roy Johnson, Jr., a visionary leader and entrepreneur, takes you on a profound exploration of how the timeless, life-changing teachings of Scripture can be harnessed to conquer the challenges of modern entrepreneurship. As you delve into the stories of biblical figures who overcame insurmountable odds, you'll find inspiration, guidance, and practical wisdom that will ultimately empower you to rise above your own obstacles.

But "Entrepreneurial Giants" is more than a collection of historical anecdotes; it's a blueprint for personal and professional growth. Dr. Roy Johnson, Jr. draws on his own experiences as a trailblazing entrepreneur to show you how to apply these ancient principles to your own journey. With each chapter, you'll gain valuable insights into decision-making, faith, unity, and the transformative power of determination.

Why should you embark on this transformative voyage? Because within these pages, you'll find the excellent tools and inspiration you need to turn isolation into community, doubt into confidence, and struggles into stepping-stones.

Whether you're just starting your entrepreneurial journey or seeking to revitalize your existing ventures, "Entrepreneurial Giants" is your steadfast companion and guide. Your entrepreneurial path is a tapestry waiting to be woven with faith, determination, and divine guidance. Let this book be your compass, your mentor, and your source of empowerment.

With every page you turn, you'll discover the groundbreaking insights that will fuel your growth and propel you toward unprecedented business breakthroughs.

So, dear reader, the foundation for your journey has been laid. Step boldly into the world of "Entrepreneurial Giants" and embrace the destiny that awaits you.

Together with Dr. Roy Johnson, Jr. and the dependable wisdom of the ages, you'll embark on an exciting adventure where faith and entrepreneurship unite to create a legacy that transcends time itself. Your breakthrough begins now.

Sonja R. Lowe, Ph.D.
Founder and President
Strategic Growth Leaders Bible University
www.SGLU.org
Founder and CEO
Sonja Lowe Coaching & Consulting
www.SonjaLowe.com

Preface

Step into a world where the echoes of history and the whispers of faith converge in "Entrepreneurial Giants: Drawing Strength from Biblical Principles for Business Breakthroughs." I introduce to you an outstanding literary masterpiece that uniquely transcends the boundaries of business wisdom and spiritual insight. "Entrepreneurial Giants: Drawing Strength from Biblical Principles for Business Breakthroughs" is not just any regular book; it's a lifeline for those navigating the deep, uncharted waters of entrepreneurship.

We know that entrepreneurship is a thrilling adventure, a journey that ignites the fires of innovation and liberation. But let's be real—this journey can also be isolating, a solitary expedition where the weight of dismissal, doubt, and discouragement can sometimes threaten to overshadow our dreams. In these moments of challenge and seclusion, we need guidance, inspiration, and a map to unconventionally navigate the turbulent terrain.

"Entrepreneurial Giants" is your compass, your beacon of hope, and your source of strength. Within its pages, you will uncover the powerful principles that unite our entrepreneurial endeavors with the timeless wisdom of the Scriptures. You will journey through stories of biblical figures who, like us, faced insurmountable adversity, doubted their abilities, and dared to rise above their circumstances.

Through the captivating narrative, you'll witness the audacity of David as he confronts Goliath, a metaphor for the giants that stand in the way of our business aspirations. You'll draw advantageous lessons from Noah and how his faith and obedience saved not only his family but also the animals and ultimately paved the way for humanity to continue.

But this book isn't just about recounting stories; it's about applying these unique stories to our modern lives. It's about weaving the threads of faith, business acumen, and divine guidance into a tapestry of success. As entrepreneurs, we are called to transcend the boundaries of our comfort zones, and "Entrepreneurial Giants" equips us with the powerful tools to do just that.

Why should you grab hold of this empowering book? Because it's not just about business; it's about transformation. It's about finding solace amid solitude and empowerment in the face of adversity. It's about awakening the entrepreneurial giant within you, that relentless spirit that refuses to succumb to challenges and setbacks.

So, my friends, if you're ready to break free from the chains of isolation and readily infuse your business journey with biblical wisdom and unwavering faith, then "Entrepreneurial Giants" is your guide. It's your ally in the battle against self-doubt, your armor in the face of day-to-day challenges, and your blueprint for unprecedented business breakthroughs.

Step into a realm where business and spirituality harmoniously converge, where the echoes of the past resonate with the demands of the present. Let "Entrepreneurial Giants" be your roadmap, your mentor, and your source of divine empowerment. Let its wisdom transform your entrepreneurial journey from a solitary expedition into a collective legacy of faith and triumph. Your breakthrough awaits, and it begins within the pages of this extraordinary book.

Table of Contents

Introduction

Courageously step into a world where the past dances with the present, where the infinite wisdom of Scripture fuses seamlessly with the unyielding power and force of entrepreneurship. Welcome to a journey that transcends mere success and redefines the fabric of your entrepreneurial aspirations. Within the pages of "Entrepreneurial Giants: Drawing Strength from Biblical Principles for Business Breakthroughs," you'll discover the far-fetched roadmap to forging unshakable foundations for your business endeavors.

Allow me to formally introduce myself. I am Dr. Roy L. Johnson, Jr., a courageous, trailblazing, highly driven, and motivated leader, author, speaker, coach, and entrepreneur with a heart set on shattering limitations. Born to a creed that preached the power of education, I transformed my passion into reality, proving that dreams are meant to be lived. With each step, I embraced challenges as opportunities, obstacles as catalysts, and adversity as fuel for ascension.

Like an uncharted sea, entrepreneurship is both exhilarating and treacherous. The waters may be rough, but it's within this turmoil that greatness emerges. In "Entrepreneurial Giants," I beckon you to join me on this voyage of self-discovery, a quest to unearth the gems hidden within the Scriptures and harness their power for business breakthroughs.

These absorbing tales of faith that reverberate throughout history are more than stories—they are blueprints for your success. As you delve into this volume, you'll witness the audacity of David confronting his Goliaths and Esther ascending to prominence against

1

all daunting odds. Through each chapter, the voices of biblical giants will resonate in harmony with your own entrepreneurial journey.

This is not a mere recounting of stories; it's a journey into the heart of biblical principles that hold the powerful keys to entrepreneurial triumph. Proverbs will guide your decision-making, faith will transform your uncertainties into stepping stones, and unity will be your launchpad to exponential growth, much like the early Church's evolution.

Why should you embark on this privileged transformative voyage? Because within these pages lies the alchemy that will transmute your isolation into communion, your doubt into certainty, and your struggles into stepping stones. As you navigate the crooked entrepreneurial highway, "Entrepreneurial Giants" will be your trustworthy, steadfast companion, systematically igniting your spirit and guiding your path.

Your entrepreneurial journey is a tapestry woven with faith, determination, and divine guidance. Let "Entrepreneurial Giants" be your steadfast guide, propelling you toward the success you deserve. With each turn of the page, you'll discover groundbreaking tools, stories, and insights that will catalyze your growth and catapult you into an era of unprecedented business breakthroughs.

Dear reader, the unique foundation for your journey has been laid—welcome to "Entrepreneurial Giants." Your breakthrough is not just a possibility; it's a destiny that awaits your embrace within these pages. Let's journey together toward an interesting future where faith and entrepreneurship converge to create a legacy that transcends the limits of time. Your thrilling adventure begins now.

Chapter 1: *Divine Favor*

Unveiling the Entrepreneurial Path of Success through Integrity and God's Presence

Genesis 39:2-3 (NKJV): "The LORD was with Joseph, and he was a successful man; and he was in the house of his master the Egyptian. And his master saw that the LORD *was* with him and that the LORD made all he did to prosper in his hand."

****

Principles in Action

Joseph, the beloved son of Jacob, was sold into slavery by his brothers out of jealousy. He ended up in Egypt, serving in the household of Potiphar, an influential Egyptian. Despite the unfair circumstances, Joseph's positive and admirable character and diligence shone through, just as Genesis 39:2-3 describes.

Joseph's outright integrity and dedication captured Potiphar's attention. The Lord's favor was evident in Joseph's life, as he consistently demonstrated excellence and grace in his work. Potiphar recognized that Joseph's success resulted from God's presence with him.

Joseph's inspiring journey in Potiphar's household exemplifies the principles of Genesis 39:2-3. Despite being a slave, Joseph prospered due to his reliance on God and commitment to his responsibilities. This story encourages entrepreneurs to maintain their integrity, even in challenging situations, and to recognize that God's presence and favor can lead to success, regardless of how helpless their circumstances might seem. Just as Joseph's unwavering faithfulness led to his elevation, entrepreneurs can trust that their dedication to

3

their work and faith in God's guidance can pave the trouble-free way for prosperity and breakthroughs.

Entrepreneurial Insights: Bridging Genesis 39:2-3 and Business

Divine Favor: Just as Joseph experienced the Lord's presence and favor in all his endeavors, entrepreneurs can find assurance that their faith and diligence can attract divine blessings. When entrepreneurs commit their work to God and seek His guidance, they can expect His favor to shine upon their efforts.

Character and Integrity: Joseph's impeccable character and integrity amid adversity set him apart. Similarly, entrepreneurs who wholly prioritize honesty, ethics, and quality in their work build a strong foundation for success. Upholding strong ethical principles, putting in consistent effort, and trustworthiness not only attract customers but also establish a credible reputation that can lead to long-term prosperity.

Recognition of Excellence: Joseph's dedication and excellence in his work caught the attention of his master, Potiphar. Similarly, entrepreneurs who consistently deliver quality products or services and go the extra mile are more likely to gain recognition and positive feedback from clients, customers, and investors.

Success Amid Challenges: Despite being a slave and facing numerous daunting challenges, Joseph thrived due to his unwavering reliance on God. Entrepreneurs often encounter obstacles and setbacks, but by maintaining a strong faith and trusting in God's provision, they can navigate difficulties with resilience and ultimately achieve success.

God as a Strategic Partner: Joseph's success was attributed to the Lord's presence. For entrepreneurs, recognizing God as a strategic planner and partner in their business journey can bring wisdom, direction, and breakthroughs beyond human capabilities.

Leadership Through Humility: Joseph's humility in serving Potiphar laid the groundwork for his later leadership. Entrepreneurs who embrace a humble attitude, valuing teamwork and learning from others, can foster a positive work environment and pave the way for rapid growth.

Encouragement in Adversity: Joseph's story encourages entrepreneurs facing discouragement, rejection, or setbacks. Just as Joseph's story took unexpected turns for good, entrepreneurs can find hope that God can use difficult situations to ultimately lead to their breakthroughs.

In essence, Genesis 39:2-3 serves as an encouraging reminder to entrepreneurs that a combination of faith, integrity, excellence, and reliance on God's guidance can lead to evident success even in challenging circumstances. By adopting these principles, entrepreneurs can navigate the entrepreneurial landscape with resilience and the expectation of God's favor in their endeavors.

Harvesting Insights: Gold Mining for Business Growth

1. How can I cultivate an environment of excellence and integrity in my business endeavors, similar to Joseph's approach in Potiphar's household, to attract recognition and favor from clients, customers, and partners?

   _____

   _____

   _____

   _____

   _____

   _____

2. In what practical ways can I acknowledge and seek God's presence and guidance in my entrepreneurial journey, trusting that His favor can lead to breakthroughs even when facing challenges and setbacks?

   _____

   _____

   _____

_____

_____

_____

_____

3. What steps can I take to demonstrate consistent dedication and commitment to my work, fostering a reputation for reliability and quality that mirrors Joseph's attitude toward his responsibilities?

_____

_____

_____

_____

_____

_____

_____

Benefits: These questions encourage entrepreneurs to reflect on their values, work ethics, and approach to their business ventures.

Cultivating Growth: Insights to Propel Your Journey

Ladies and gentlemen, let me introduce you to Ethan, the tenacious entrepreneur with a heart of gold and a tenacious spirit that refused to be broken.

Meet Ethan, a young visionary who embarked on a mission to revolutionize the tech world. He founded "Innovate Tech Inc.," a startup with a mission to marry innovation with social impact. Armed with codes and compassion, Ethan was on a quest to change lives, one byte at a time.

But the journey wasn't all rainbows and algorithms. Ethan faced hurdles that would've made most retreat. Amid his struggles, he stumbled upon Genesis 39:2-3 – "The Lord was with Joseph, and he was a successful man; and he was in the house of his master the Egyptian. And his master saw that the Lord was with him and that the Lord made all he did to prosper in his hand."

With a satirical smile, Ethan embraced and held onto these verses like a secret weapon. He realized that God's presence was his ultimate algorithm for success. It was about being a beacon of integrity in a world where shortcuts tempted like sirens.

One day, as Ethan presented his game-changing app that connected underserved communities to vital resources, he faced a panel of skeptics who questioned the practicality of his vision. But Ethan stood like a solid rock, driven not just by lines of code but by the promise of Genesis 39:2-3.

His presentation was a blend of passion and purpose, of numbers and nobility. Slowly, skepticism melted into awe, and before Ethan knew it, he'd secured the partnership that would take "Innovate Tech Inc." to new heights.

As news of Ethan's triumph spread, his startup transformed from a small idea to a tech giant with a heart. Ethan's name became synonymous with innovation and impact; his app was celebrated as a game-changer in the industry.

As Ethan looked at the horizon of endless possibility, he marveled at the truth of Genesis 39:2-3. Like Joseph, he realized that his faithfulness wasn't just for personal gain but a force that could catalyze progress and prosperity.

And so, "Innovate Tech Inc." continued to flourish, not just as a business but as a movement of conscience-driven innovation. Ethan's story was a living testament that when God's presence is your co-founder, your vision isn't limited by algorithms; it's powered by providence.

So, my friends, let Ethan's journey continually remind you that success isn't just about what you do; it's about who's with you. When the world challenges your integrity or doubts your vision, remember Genesis 39:2-3 – it's your assurance that faithfulness attracts favor. By aligning your purpose with God's presence, you'll prosper not just in business but in leaving a legacy of impact that transcends the binary code of commerce.

Chapter 2: *Rooted Prosperity*

Thriving Through Faithful Trust in Seasons of Entrepreneurial Growth

Jeremiah 17:7-8 (NKJV): "But blessed is the one who trusts in the LORD, whose confidence is in him. They will be like a tree planted by the water that sends out its roots by the stream. It does not fear when heat comes; its leaves are always green. It has no worries in a year of drought and never fails to bear fruit."

****

Principles in Action

Originally known as Abram, Abraham was called by God to leave his homeland and go to a place God would show him. In Genesis 12, God promised to bless Abram and make him a great nation. Despite not knowing where he was going, Abram wholly trusted God and embarked on this uncertain journey.

As the years went by, Abram faced various daunting challenges and uncertainties. He experienced moments of doubt, yet he remained steadfast in trusting God's promises. In Genesis 15, God reaffirmed His covenant with Abram, promising him descendants as numerous as the stars.

In due time, God fulfilled His promise, and Abram became Abraham, the father of many nations. Despite their old age, he and his wife, Sarah, bore a son, Isaac. Abraham's faith in God's promises, even during times of drought and uncertainty, led to immeasurable blessings.

Connection to Jeremiah 17:7-8

The story of Abraham reflects the principles found in Jeremiah 17:7-8. Just as the tree by the water flourishes and remains steadfast through various seasons, Abraham's complete trust in God's promises allowed him to thrive despite discouraging challenges and uncertainties. His unwavering faith led to a legacy of blessings and prosperity, demonstrating the truth of Jeremiah 17:7-8 in his life.

Entrepreneurs can draw divine inspiration from Abraham's story, understanding that when they place their trust in the Lord and remain rooted in faith, their entrepreneurial journey can weather any challenges that come their way. Like the tree by the water, their businesses can remain resilient, fruitful, and prosperous, regardless of external circumstances.

Abraham's solid faith and unwavering trust in the Lord permitted him to overcome seemingly insurmountable obstacles and achieve an exceedingly generous amount of success. Similarly, entrepreneurs who maintain their faith and trust in their abilities can find the fortitude to persevere through turbulent times and ultimately thrive in their entrepreneurial endeavors.

Entrepreneurial Insights: Bridging Jeremiah 17:7-8 and Business

Trust and Confidence: Just as the verse emphasizes completely trusting in the Lord and having confidence in Him, entrepreneurs are reminded to, without doubt, trust God's guidance and provision. This trust becomes the cornerstone of their decision-making and strategy, offering a steadying force amid uncertainties. By placing their faith in a higher purpose and seeking guidance, they can navigate ominous challenges with a sense of assurance and stability.

Rooted Resilience: Entrepreneurs, like the tree by the water, need to establish their businesses on a solid foundation. When they root themselves in ethical practices, a strong work ethic, and strong values that align with God's principles, they can withstand challenges and remain steadfast even during difficult times.

Flourishing through Adversity: The image of a tree with green leaves despite heat and drought mirrors entrepreneurs' ability to thrive despite challenges. By relying on God and adapting their strategies, they can continue to innovate and find growth opportunities, even in challenging and uncertain market conditions.

Trees endure diverse seasons, and entrepreneurs can similarly persist through the ups and downs of business. Consistent effort, even during challenging times, can yield long-term growth and resilience, mirroring the tree's ability to withstand drought.

Enduring Fruitfulness: Just as the tree never fails to bear fruit, entrepreneurs who nurture their businesses with dedication and perseverance can expect their efforts to yield rewarding results over time. Consistency, commitment, and a focus on long-term impact can lead to sustainable success.

Freedom from Fear: Entrepreneurs often face uncertainties and risks. However, when their trust is in God, they can move forward without the burden of fear. Trusting in God's master plan and providence allows entrepreneurs to make bold decisions unencumbered by anxieties.

Confidence in God's Timing: Jeremiah 17:7-8 implies a resilience that arises from a deep-rooted relationship with God. In the same way, entrepreneurs can also find assurance that their efforts, when guided by faith and patience, will bear rewarding fruit in due time, aligning with God's divine timing.

Just as trees bear fruit in due season, entrepreneurs can set milestones and celebrate achievements along their journey. By measuring progress, setting goals, and acknowledging their accomplishments, entrepreneurs can maintain consistent motivation and a sense of purpose.

Sustained Growth: Just as the tree's roots reach the water source, entrepreneurs are encouraged to stay connected to the divine sources of knowledge, mentorship, and wisdom. This continuous learning and spiritual nourishment can ultimately foster sustained growth and development. Embracing a growth mindset and keeping your mind open like a parachute to new ideas can lead to innovation and sustained success.

Fundamentally, Jeremiah 17:7-8 empowers and motivates entrepreneurs to cultivate a mindset of trust, resilience, and faith as they navigate the dynamic business landscape. By being intentional and firmly aligning their actions with these principles, entrepreneurs can boldly and confidently find strength in their journey, regardless of the challenges they encounter, and experience the bountiful fulfillment of their entrepreneurial aspirations.

Harvesting Insights: Gold Mining for Business Growth

1. How can I intentionally cultivate a consistent business culture that prioritizes trust in God's guidance, both in decision-making and in fostering relationships with clients, partners, and employees, as highlighted in Jeremiah 17:7-8?

_____

_____

_____

_____

_____

_____

2. In what ways can I ensure that my entrepreneurial endeavors are firmly rooted in ethical practices and values strictly aligned with God's principles, so that my business remains resilient and fruitful despite challenges, mirroring the imagery of the tree by the water?

_____

_____

_____

_____

_____

_____

_____

_____

3. What strategies can I implement to balance proactive adaptation with patient endurance, recognizing that sustained success often aligns with the idea that entrepreneurial efforts, when guided by unwavering faith, can yield lasting results over time, like the enduring fruitfulness portrayed in Jeremiah 17:7-8?

_____

_____

_____

_____

_____

_____

_____

Benefits: These questions encourage entrepreneurs to critically assess their business practices, values, and mindset, allowing them to draw deeper insights and actionable takeaways.

Cultivating Growth: Insights to Propel Your Journey

Ladies and gentlemen, brace yourselves! Your soul is about to be ignited, and seeds of inspiration are about to be planted. Allow me to introduce you to Emily, the spirited entrepreneur who danced to her own beat and defied the odds.

Meet Emily, a whirlwind of passion and grit. She started "Roots & Wings Enterprises," a venture rooted in sustainability and innovation. With a heart full of dreams and a head full of determination, Emily aimed to change the world, one eco-friendly product at a time.

But oh, the path was no leisurely stroll. Emily faced skeptics who dismissed her green initiatives as a pipe dream. Amidst the cynicism, she stumbled upon Jeremiah 17:7-8 – "Blessed is the man who trusts in the Lord, whose confidence is in Him. He will be like a tree planted by the water that sends out its roots by the stream."

With a grin as wide as her dreams, Emily confidently embraced these verses like a lifeline. She understood that trusting in God was like nurturing roots that could withstand any storm. It was about being an unshakable force in the face of doubt.

One pivotal day, as Emily presented her eco-friendly products to a skeptical group of investors, she felt the weight of their doubts. But with the verses of Jeremiah echoing in her heart, Emily stood tall like the very tree she aimed to emulate.

Her pitch was a symphony of passion, innovation, and unyielding faith. Slowly, skepticism gave way to curiosity, and by the time Emily was done, the room was buzzing with excitement. Investors saw not just a business proposal but a formidable vision that could reshape industries.

As news of Emily's success spread, "Roots & Wings Enterprises" evolved from a fledgling venture to an influential movement. Emily's name became synonymous with courage, her products revered, and her journey celebrated as the embodiment of Jeremiah 17:7-8.

As Emily stood amidst a forest of her creations, she marveled at the depth of Jeremiah's wisdom. She realized that wholeheartedly trusting in God was the fertile ground on which she'd built her empire. Just as a tree flourished by the stream, Emily flourished by her faith.

And so, "Roots & Wings Enterprises" continued to thrive as a business and a living testament to the power of unwavering trust. Emily's journey was a beacon, reminding us that when you fully trust in God, you become unshakeable like the roots of a tree.

So, my friends, let Emily's journey be a compass for your dreams. When doubts cast shadows and obstacles seem insurmountable, remember Jeremiah 17:7-8 – it's your anchor in the storm. By trusting in God, your roots will run deep, your confidence unwavering, and, like Emily's, your journey will be a story of blessed success, standing tall like a tree planted by the waters of faith.

Chapter 3: *Champions of Diligence*

Unlocking Success through Proactive Excellence

Proverbs 22:29 (NKJV): "Do you see someone skilled in their work? They will serve before kings; they will not serve before officials of low rank."

****

Principles in Action

Daniel was a young man from Judah who was taken into captivity in Babylon. Despite his circumstances, he demonstrated exceptional qualities of wisdom, intelligence, and skill. In Daniel 1, he and his friends were chosen to serve in King Nebuchadnezzar's court due to their excellence.

One instance that showcases Daniel's profound skill and wisdom is found in Daniel 2. The king had a dream that troubled him, and he sought an interpretation. Relying on God's revelation, Daniel was able to interpret the dream and provide a solution to the king's concerns. Impressed by Daniel's abilities, King Nebuchadnezzar promoted him to a position of authority.

Daniel's continued excellence led him to serve multiple kings, including King Darius. He was known for his integrity, wisdom, and administrative abilities. His skillful leadership extended even to handling political intrigue, as seen in the story of the lions' den (Daniel 6).

Connection to Proverbs 22:29

Daniel's journey aligns with the wisdom of Proverbs 22:29. His exceptional skills and wisdom set him apart, allowing him to serve before kings and leaders of the highest rank. His diligent and skillful service earned him positions of influence and opportunities to impact nations and even influence policies.

From Daniel's story, entrepreneurs can learn that cultivating skills, wisdom, and excellence in their work can lead to remarkable opportunities and recognition. Just as Daniel's skills elevated him to serve before kings, entrepreneurs who demonstrate exceptional proficiency in their respective fields can divinely gain access to influential circles and positions of authority, enabling them to make a significant impact.

Daniel's story reinforces the timeless truth of Proverbs 22:29 by showcasing the rewards of skillful and diligent work that stands out before those in high positions. Entrepreneurs are encouraged to hone their abilities and contribute their talents with excellence, as this can fundamentally open doors to remarkable opportunities and platforms for impact.

Entrepreneurial Insights: Bridging Proverbs 22:29 and Business

Skill and Excellence: Just as the verse emphasizes the importance of being skilled in one's work, entrepreneurs are encouraged to continually improve their God-given skills and strive for excellence in their chosen fields. Developing expertise and delivering high-quality products or services benefits their business and positions them for recognition and success. Additionally, by honing their skills and expertise, they can become indispensable and excel in their chosen field, much like someone skilled in their work.

Opportunities for Influence: The promise of serving before kings speaks to entrepreneurs' potential to gain access to influential networks and platforms. Entrepreneurs who excel in their work can attract attention from industry leaders, potential investors, and decision-makers, providing opportunities to influence, collaborate, and make a lasting impact.

Recognition and Advancement: Entrepreneurs who stand out through their proficiency and dedication can expect to be recognized and rewarded. Just as the skilled worker's service is not relegated to low-ranking officials, entrepreneurs who demonstrate exceptional abilities will likely be elevated in their industry, fostering career advancement and growth.

Marketplace Leadership: The verse underscores the concept of recognizing and promoting talent. Entrepreneurs who demonstrate competence and innovation can become leaders within their market niche, guiding their industry's direction and setting new standards for others to follow.

Positive Reputation: Skillful entrepreneurs not only excel in their work but also earn a reputation for reliability and trustworthiness. As they consistently deliver quality solutions, their reputation grows, attracting loyal customers, partners, and collaborators.

Long-Term Success: By prioritizing skill development and striving for excellence, entrepreneurs lay a solid foundation for sustained success. Their dedication to continuous improvement ensures that their offerings remain relevant, valuable, and competitive over time.

Personal Fulfillment: Embracing skillful work and achieving excellence brings personal satisfaction and a sense of purpose. Entrepreneurs who invest in honing their abilities find fulfillment in contributing meaningfully to their field and positively impacting their customers and society.

Innately, Proverbs 22:29 serves as a motivational reminder for everyday entrepreneurs to pursue skillful, excellent work, surpassing mediocrity mentally, thus standing out among others. By doing so, they can anticipate recognition, access influential circles, and make significant contributions that extend beyond their immediate business endeavors, thereby inspiring others to follow in their footsteps, creating meaningful change, making an unforgettable embedded impact, establishing themselves as a true champion in their field, and leaving a permeating legacy in their industry and the world.

Harvesting Insights: Gold Mining for Business Growth

1. How can I intentionally invest in improving and refining my skills within my industry, recognizing that skillfulness is a gateway to both personal growth and gaining access to influential circles, as emphasized in Proverbs 22:29?

_____

_____

_____

_____

_____

_____

2. In what ways can I strategically position myself and my business to showcase my expertise and skillfulness, understanding that standing out in my field can lead to rewarding opportunities for collaboration, influence, and leadership, echoing the concept of serving before kings?

_____

_____

_____

_____

_____

_____

_____

_____

3. What steps can I take to ensure that my commitment to skill development is consistently reflected in the quality of products or services I provide, aligning with Proverbs 22:29's idea that skillful work leads to recognition and advancement rather than serving low-ranking officials?

_____

_____

_____

_____

_____

_____

_____

Benefits: These questions encourage entrepreneurs to critically assess their commitment to skill development, positioning within their industry, and the quality of their offerings.

Cultivating Growth: Insights to Propel Your Journey

Ladies and gentlemen, are you ready for your ambition to be jolted? Allow me to introduce you to Max, the embodiment of hustle and heart.

Meet Max, the go-getter who believed that the sky was just a starting point. He kicked off his venture, "Momentum Makers Inc.," with a mission to redefine success. Max's energy was infectious, his ideas boundless, and his potential limitless.

But the road to triumph wasn't a straight highway. Max faced discouraging potholes of doubt, detours of setbacks, and traffic jams of naysayers. Amid the chaos, Max stumbled upon Proverbs 22:29 – "Do you see a man skilled in his work? He will serve before kings; he will not serve before obscure men."

With a grin as wide as his dreams, Max internalized this wisdom. He knew that being skilled wasn't just about talent; it was about unwavering dedication, the kind that could turn a pebble into a diamond.

One day, as Max presented his innovative idea to a room full of investors, a hushed excitement filled the air. The boardroom felt like a battlefield, and Max was the fearless general. Armed with his dedication and the knowledge that his work was his ticket to greatness, he delivered a pitch that left everyone in awe.

Investors leaned in, skepticism transformed into fascination, and before Max knew it, his "Momentum Makers" had secured the partnership that would change the game.

As news of Max's triumph spread, his venture transformed from a startup to a proficient powerhouse. Max's name became synonymous with excellence, his ideas revered, and his story celebrated as the modern-day embodiment of Proverbs 22:29.

As Max stood among the giants of industry, he marveled at the truth in Proverbs 22:29. He understood that skill was the divine compass that guided him through the wilderness of doubt. Just as a craftsman's hands shape raw materials into masterpieces, Max's dedication transformed his ideas into reality.

And so, "Momentum Makers Inc." continued to soar, not just as a business but as an encouraging reminder that dedication could move mountains. Max's story became a testament to the fact that the journey from obscurity to greatness was paved with a relentless pursuit of excellence.

So, my friends, let Max's journey inspire you. When doubt creeps in, and setbacks try to divert your path, remember Proverbs 22:29 – it's your compass to success. By diligently honing your skills, dedicating yourself to your craft, and believing in the transformative power of hard work, you can navigate your way to the halls of greatness. Because, as Max knew, a man skilled in his work would serve before kings, and his journey from obscurity to prominence would be a tale worth celebrating.

Chapter 4: *Limitless Strength*

Embracing Victory Through Christ's Empowerment

Philippians 4:13 (NKJV): "I can do all things through Christ who strengthens me."

****

Principles in Action

The story of David and Goliath in 1 Samuel 17 illustrates the principles found in Philippians 4:13.

The Philistine army was at war with the Israelites, and they had a champion warrior named Goliath who challenged the Israelites to send out a champion to fight him in single combat. No Israelite was brave enough to face him until David, a young shepherd, arrived.

Understand this: There will be many times in your life and business when you will feel like giving up. Or feel like quitting or throwing in the towel. You may even start feeling like you've been violated, stripped down to nothing, and emasculated instead of being built up by the ones who are supposed to be on your side. Despite the situation, will you buckle under the pressure, or will you RISE UP to the occasion?

See, the Bible says, David got up, armed with only a sling and five stones, ran into the army of the Philistines, and faced the formidable Goliath. Despite his opponent's massive size and strength, David's faith and confidence in God were unshaken. He declared to Goliath that he came in the name of the Lord Almighty, knowing that God would empower him to overcome the giant.

With a single stone hurled from his sling, David struck Goliath in the forehead, and Goliath fell. Despite all odds, David's faith and trust in God's strength led to an astonishing victory.

Entrepreneurial Insights: Bridging Philippians 4:13 and Business

David's story reflects the essence of Philippians 4:13. Just as David faced the seemingly insurmountable challenge of Goliath, he drew strength from his unwavering faith in God. His proclamation that he could do all things through God's empowerment aligns with the spirit of Philippians 4:13.

Entrepreneurs can learn from David's story that, like him, they can confidently face seemingly impossible challenges when they draw strength from God. Just as David's faith empowered him to triumph over a giant, entrepreneurs who trust in God's strength can overcome obstacles, surpass limitations, and achieve remarkable victories in their entrepreneurial endeavors.

David's story exemplifies the truth of Philippians 4:13 by illustrating the transformative power of faith and God's empowerment in overcoming challenges that may seem insurmountable. Entrepreneurs can take inspiration from this story to approach their business challenges with confidence, knowing that through God's strength, they can achieve remarkable success.

1. How can I actively integrate the belief that I can do all things through Christ's empowerment into my daily business practices, decision-making, and attitude, as outlined in Philippians 4:13?

   _____

   _____

   _____

   _____

   _____

   _____

   _____

2. In what ways can I leverage the strength derived from Christ's empowerment to overcome specific challenges or limitations I'm currently facing in my entrepreneurial journey, aligning with the spirit of Philippians 4:13?

   _____

   _____

   _____

_____

_____

_____

_____

3. What strategies can I implement to cultivate a resilient and empowered mindset within my team, instilling the belief that, collectively, we can overcome obstacles and achieve success through Christ's strength, in accordance with Philippians 4:13?

_____

_____

_____

_____

_____

_____

_____

Benefits: These questions encourage entrepreneurs to critically reflect on their faith-based perspective, strategies for overcoming challenges, and leadership approach.

Cultivating Growth: Insights to Propel Your Journey

Ladies and gentlemen, fasten your seatbelts for a story that'll ignite your spirit and spark your determination. Allow me to introduce you to Lily, the spirited entrepreneur with dreams as big as her heart.

Meet Lily, a whirlwind of ambition and enthusiasm. She started "Dreams Unleashed Inc.," an empire built on turning visions into reality. With a twinkle in her eye and a bounce in her step, Lily believed that nothing was impossible.

But life wasn't all sunshine and rainbows. The path to success was more like a rollercoaster, complete with exhilarating highs and nerve-wracking drops. Amid challenges, Lily discovered Philippians 4:13 – "I can do all things through Christ who strengthens me."

With a grin that could light up a room, Lily embraced this verse like a superhero's cape. She realized that her determination, fueled by divine strength, could conquer any daunting obstacle in her way.

One day, as Lily was battling her fiercest competitor for a game-changing contract, doubt threatened to derail her. She remembered Philippians 4:13 and, with a heart full of faith, channeled her inner superhero. With every pitch and presentation, Lily tapped into a strength beyond her own, a strength that made her unstoppable.

The competition was fierce, and the stakes were high, but Lily's unyielding spirit and unwavering belief set her apart. And just like that, she secured the contract that would redefine her company's trajectory.

As news of Lily's victory spread, "Dreams Unleashed Inc." transformed from a promising venture to a formidable industry titan.

Lily's name became synonymous with tenacity and triumph, inspiring others to dream big and reach for the stars.

Lily marveled at the wisdom of Philippians 4:13. She understood that her own limitations were mere illusions in the face of divine empowerment. Just as a marathon runner relies on the cheering crowd for that final burst of energy, Lily relied on Christ's strength to push her beyond her perceived limits.

And so, "Dreams Unleashed Inc." continued to flourish as a business and a beacon of hope. Lily's story was a living testament that with Christ's strength, ordinary individuals could achieve extraordinary feats.

So, my friends, let Lily's journey remind you that life's challenges are mere stepping stones to greatness. When the odds are stacked against you, remember Philippians 4:13 – it's your secret weapon, your ticket to soaring beyond your wildest dreams. With Christ's advantageous strength, you can conquer mountains, shatter ceilings, and achieve the unimaginable. Because, as Lily discovered, through Christ, you can truly do all things.

Chapter 5: *Mastering the Small to Seize the Grand*

Unleashing Abundance through Faithful Stewardship

Luke 16:10 (NKJV): "He who is faithful in what is least is faithful also in much; and he who is unjust in what is least is unjust also in much."

****

Principles in Action

The story of the widow's offering in Mark 12:41-44 critically illustrates the principles found in Luke 16:10.

In the temple, Jesus observed people placing their offerings into the treasury. Many wealthy people gave large sums, but a poor widow came and put in two small coins, which were worth only a fraction of a penny.

Jesus, recognizing the widow's sacrificial heart, praised her actions. He explained that while the wealthy gave out of their abundance, the widow gave all she had. Her small offering held great significance because it represented her complete trust in God's provision.

Connection to Luke 16:10

The story of the widow's offering embodies the essence of Luke 16:10. The widow's willingness to faithfully give from what little she had exemplifies the principle of being faithful in little things. Her small offering, when seen through the lens of her sincere heart, held immense value in the eyes of God.

Application to Everyday Life

Entrepreneurs can learn a life-changing lesson from the widow's story by understanding that faithful stewardship extends beyond financial matters. Just as she entrusted God with her small offering, entrepreneurs are encouraged to faithfully steward their resources, time, talents, and opportunities. No matter how seemingly insignificant, every action can have far-reaching effects when approached with sincerity and faithfulness.

Entrepreneurs who prioritize faithful stewardship in both their personal and professional lives demonstrate integrity and a commitment to honoring God. By being faithful in small matters, entrepreneurs lay the foundation for greater responsibilities and blessings, in line with the principles outlined in Luke 16:10.

Entrepreneurial Insights: Bridging Luke 16:10 and Business

Integrity in Small Matters: The verse underscores the importance of integrity in small matters. For entrepreneurs, this means consistently adhering to ethical standards and making honest decisions, even in seemingly insignificant situations. Such consistency immensely builds a reputation of trustworthiness that extends to larger matters.

Trustworthiness in Finances: Entrepreneurs often deal with financial matters of varying scales. By demonstrating unwavering trustworthiness in managing even modest resources, entrepreneurs establish a foundation of credibility that can attract investors, partners, and clients who value responsible financial management.

Commitment to Excellence: Entrepreneurs who apply the principle of faithfulness in small tasks show their complete commitment and dedication to excellence. This can influence the quality of their products or services, setting them apart in competitive markets and fostering customer loyalty.

Nurturing Relationships: Small acts of kindness and attentive communication tremendously contribute to nurturing relationships. Entrepreneurs who value these gestures create a supportive network that can prove invaluable in times of need or for business growth.

Learning and Growth: Faithfulness in learning and personal growth is vital. Entrepreneurs who consistently seek knowledge and self-improvement, even in small increments, position themselves for more significant advancements and innovations in the long run.

Consistency in Work Ethic: Entrepreneurs who maintain a strong work ethic in both large and small tasks exhibit a reliable dedication to their goals. This diligence can lead to a culture of persistence that benefits their businesses and teams.

Godly Character: Entrepreneurs who integrate principles of faithfulness and integrity reflect godly character. This can advantageously attract like-minded partners and collaborators, fostering an environment that aligns with their values and contributes to long-term success.

To bring it home, Luke 16:10 encourages everyday entrepreneurs to recognize that their actions in small matters have a far-reaching impact on their overall success. By prioritizing faithfulness and integrity in all aspects of their entrepreneurial journey, entrepreneurs lay a foundation for growth, influence, and a legacy built on principles that resonate with both customers and partners.

Harvesting Insights: Gold Mining for Business Growth

1. How can I evaluate my current business practices to identify instances where I've demonstrated faithfulness and integrity in small matters, and how have these instances contributed to building a foundation of trust and credibility within my industry?

   _____

   _____

   _____

   _____

   _____

   _____

   _____

2. In what ways can I proactively apply the principle of faithfulness to my daily routines and interactions, recognizing that consistent acts of integrity in both personal and business matters can lead to long-term positive outcomes, as highlighted in Luke 16:10?

   _____

   _____

   _____

_____

_____

_____

_____

_____

3. What strategies can I implement to instill a culture of faithfulness and meticulous attention to detail within my team, fostering an environment where each member understands the significance of their contributions to the business's overall success, in alignment with Luke 16:10?

_____

_____

_____

_____

_____

_____

_____

Benefits: These questions encourage entrepreneurs to critically reflect on their adherence to principles of faithfulness and integrity, their influence on their team's culture, and their overall impact on business growth.

Cultivating Growth: Insights to Propel Your Journey

Ladies and gentlemen, steel yourselves for this educating story. Let me introduce you to Charlie, the savvy entrepreneur with a knack for turning pennies into prosperity.

Meet Charlie, the embodiment of the phrase "penny-pincher extraordinaire." He founded "Nickel Nest Enterprises," a company built on the belief that every cent counted. Charlie's friends would jokingly call him "Mr. Thrifty," but his success spoke louder than any teasing.

But, oh, the journey wasn't all smooth sailing. In the early days of "Nickel Nest," Charlie would dive into dumpsters to retrieve discarded office supplies. One fateful day, he found Luke 16:10 scribbled on a tattered notebook page among the junk – "Whoever can be trusted with very little can also be trusted with much."

With a chuckle, Charlie turned this verse into his mantra, transforming it from dusty pages to dynamic action. He realized that faithfulness in the small things was the key to unlocking bigger blessings.

One evening, as Charlie was sorting through his desk drawers (you never know what treasures you'll find!), he stumbled upon an old contract he had almost thrown away. The contract, a seemingly insignificant deal from years ago, held a clause that could be leveraged to strike a lucrative partnership with a major player in the industry.

With a knowing grin, Charlie picked up the phone and dialed the number. Negotiations ensued, and what started as a small deal turned into a game-changing alliance, propelling "Nickel Nest Enterprises" to new heights.

The partnership flourished, turning "Nickel Nest" into a household name synonymous with shrewd business acumen. Charlie's friends stopped calling him "Mr. Thrifty" and started seeking his advice on financial matters.

As "Nickel Nest Enterprises" soared, Charlie pondered Luke 16:10. He realized that being trustworthy in small matters had unlocked doors to significant opportunities. Just as a master entrusts his servant with a little before giving more responsibility, Charlie understood that faithfulness isn't just a virtue but also a strategy for success.

And so, the "Nickel Nest" story became a beacon, reminding us that greatness doesn't always start with grand gestures. Sometimes, it begins with valuing the "nickels" of life – the seemingly insignificant choices and tasks that lay the foundation for larger triumphs.

So, my friends, let Charlie's tale be a lesson that every little effort matters; every penny saved counts. When you honor the small steps, the universe conspires to make the big leaps possible. As Luke 16:10 whispered through the ages, the more faithful you are with little, the more you'll be trusted with much. And in that truth lies the secret to turning mere pennies into profound prosperity.

Chapter 6: *Seize the Winds of Opportunity*

Navigating Risk with Faith and Courage

Ecclesiastes 11:6 (KNJV): "In the morning sow your seed, and in the evening do not withhold your hand; For you do not know which will prosper, either this or that,
Or whether both alike *will be* good."

****

Principles in Action

The story of Noah and the Ark in Genesis 6-9 profoundly illustrates the principles found in Ecclesiastes 11:6.

God saw the wickedness of humanity and decided to bring a flood to cleanse the earth. He chose Noah, a righteous man, and instructed him to build an ark to save himself, his family, and two of every kind of animal.

Noah faced a significant challenge—building a massive ark on dry land, preparing for a flood that had never been seen before. Despite the lack of rain and the doubts of those around him, Noah trusted God's instructions and persevered in building the ark.

When the flood came, the ark protected Noah, his family, and the animals. After the waters receded, they emerged to a renewed world. Noah's faith and obedience saved not only his family but also the animals and ultimately paved the way for humanity to continue.

Connection to Ecclesiastes 11:6

The story of Noah and the Ark aligns with the spirit of Ecclesiastes 11:6. Noah faced a decision with uncertain outcomes—to build an ark in anticipation of a flood that hadn't yet arrived. He cast his bread upon the waters, taking a risk and investing his efforts without immediate rewards.

Application to Everyday Life

Entrepreneurs can learn from Noah's story by recognizing that taking calculated risks and stepping into the unknown can lead to remarkable outcomes. Just as Noah acted with faith and courage, entrepreneurs can embark on innovative ventures, launch new products, or enter new markets, even when outcomes are uncertain.

By "casting their bread upon the waters," entrepreneurs understand that their efforts might not yield instant results, but faith-driven actions can set the stage for future success. Similarly to how Noah's obedience led to salvation and renewal, entrepreneurs' calculated risks can lead to immense growth, transformation, and unforeseen opportunities.

The story of Noah and the Ark perfectly exemplifies the principles of Ecclesiastes 11:6 by highlighting the significance of taking risks, acting in faith, and understanding that the ventures undertaken today can yield rewards that extend beyond the immediate horizon. Entrepreneurs are encouraged to embrace calculated risks and venture into uncharted territories, knowing that their efforts can lead to positive outcomes in due time.

Entrepreneurial Insights: Bridging Ecclesiastes 11:6 and Business

Embracing Opportunity: The verse encourages entrepreneurs to take advantage of opportunities when they arise. Just as farmers sow their seeds regardless of the weather, entrepreneurs should be proactive in seizing moments for growth and innovation, even in uncertain times.

Calculated Risks: The concept of casting one's bread upon the waters resonates with entrepreneurial risk-taking. Entrepreneurs often need to invest time, resources, and effort without immediate guarantees of success. This verse reminds them that calculated risks can lead to exceedingly rewarding outcomes.

Investing in Growth: Entrepreneurs who continually seek improvement and expansion relate to the idea of diversifying their ventures. By exploring new markets, products, or strategies, entrepreneurs strategically position themselves for long-term growth and adaptability.

Delaying Gratification: The verse implies patience and delayed gratification. Entrepreneurs might not see immediate returns on their investments or efforts, but a persevering approach can yield more substantial benefits over time.

Faith in Action: Casting one's bread implies complete faith in future outcomes. Similarly, entrepreneurs operate with a degree of faith in their business endeavors. This verse reminds them to have faith that their efforts will eventually yield positive results, even if they are not immediately evident.

Boldness in Innovation: The verse's agricultural analogy reflects the courage to innovate. Entrepreneurs who pioneer new ideas, products, or services are akin to sowing seeds in uncharted territories, with the potential for future growth and impact.

Resilience in Uncertainty: Like farmers relying on unpredictable weather, entrepreneurs often face uncertainty. Ecclesiastes 11:6 encourages a resilient mindset, reminding them to press continually forward with diligence, regardless of external conditions.

Ecclesiastes 11:6 guides everyday entrepreneurs to embrace opportunities, take calculated risks, invest in growth, and maintain a steadfast attitude, even when results are not immediate. By obediently casting their efforts upon the waters of opportunity, entrepreneurs can foster long-term success, adaptability, and a positive impact on their ventures and beyond.

Harvesting Insights: Gold Mining for Business Growth

1. How can I properly identify and evaluate potential opportunities within my industry or market, and what strategies can I implement to proactively seize these opportunities, aligning with the principle of "sowing" in Ecclesiastes 11:6?

    _____

    _____

    _____

    _____

    _____

    _____

    _____

2. In what ways can I balance the need for calculated risk-taking with the necessity of making informed decisions in my entrepreneurial endeavors, ensuring that I'm effectively "casting my bread upon the waters" for future growth and success?

    _____

    _____

    _____

_____

_____

_____

_____

_____

3. What strategic measures can I implement to cultivate
    patience and resilience in the face of uncertainty or delayed
    outcomes, recognizing that the principle of Ecclesiastes 11:6
    requires a balanced approach between investing efforts now
    and patiently waiting for potential returns in the future?

_____

_____

_____

_____

_____

_____

_____

Benefits: These questions encourage entrepreneurs to critically assess their approach to seizing opportunities, managing risk, and cultivating patience.

Cultivating Growth: Insights to Propel Your Journey

Ladies and gentlemen, buckle up! Your imagination is about to go for a ride and possibly nudge your contemplative side. Allow me to introduce you to Max, the daredevil entrepreneur with a twinkle in his eye and a penchant for pushing boundaries.

Meet Max, the entrepreneurial maverick who dreamed of launching a company that'd send rockets to the moon, of all places. Yes, you heard that right – a moonshot venture! Armed with a mix of optimism and sheer audacity, Max launched "Galaxy Dreams Inc." to make his out-of-this-world vision a reality.

But, oh, the road was anything but smooth. Rocket science is tough, and Max found himself facing fiery mishaps and not-so-pretty explosions. Despite the setbacks, he'd shrug, flash a grin, and quip, "Who needs eyebrows anyway?"

As the tension between aspiration and reality mounted, Max found solace in Ecclesiastes 11:6 – a verse he stumbled upon while juggling schematics and safety protocols. It talked about sowing seeds in the morning and not withholding your hand in the evening. Max realized he couldn't just wish upon a star; he had to faithfully launch his rockets despite the risks.

One fateful evening, as stars twinkled above, Max stood before a massive rocket named "Lunar Luminary." A skeptical crowd had gathered, eyebrows raised higher than ever. Max's moment had arrived. "Let's light this candle," he grinned, quoting the legendary astronaut, Alan Shepard.

With the press of a button, Lunar Luminary roared to life. The crowd gasped as it soared toward the sky, leaving behind a trail of fire and wonder. Max's heart pounded like a drumbeat, knowing that his audacious vision was finally soaring among the stars.

Days turned into weeks, and Lunar Luminary sailed through the cosmic expanse, collecting data and beaming back images that left scientists and dreamers alike in awe. Powered by his unwavering audacity, Max's crazy dream was touching the heavens.

As Lunar Luminary returned to Earth, Max stood among a crowd of believers, eyes twinkling brighter than the stars. He realized that Ecclesiastes 11:6 had become more than words – it was a divine guiding principle. Just as a farmer sows seeds with hope in the morning and doesn't withhold his hand in the evening, Max had sown seeds of audacity and risk, reaping a harvest of innovation and inspiration.

And so, "Galaxy Dreams Inc." continued to shoot for the stars, not deterred by failures or skeptics. Max's story became a beacon, continually reminding us that sometimes, the only way to reach the moon is by boldly launching ourselves toward it.

So, my friends, let Max's journey be a testament that life rewards those who, with faith, embrace risk, who seize the morning and never withhold their hand in the evening. When your dreams are as audacious as a rocket ride to the moon, remember Ecclesiastes 11:6 – it's a reminder that audacity isn't just a trait; it's a launching pad to galaxies of possibility.

Chapter 7: *Fear Not, Rise Strong*

Harnessing God's Power in the Entrepreneurial Journey

Isaiah 41:10 (NKJV): "Fear not, for I am with you; Be not dismayed, for I am your God. I will strengthen you, yes, I will help you, I will uphold you with My righteous right hand."

****

Principles in Action

The story of Moses leading the Israelites out of Egypt and crossing the Red Sea in Exodus 14 illustrates the principles found in Isaiah 41:10.

When the Israelites found themselves trapped between the pursuing Egyptian army and the Red Sea, fear and panic spread among them. Guided by his faith in God in this dire situation, Moses demonstrated courage and trust. God's presence and intervention were evident as He instructed Moses to raise his staff and part the waters of the Red Sea.

With the sea divided into two walls of water, the Israelites walked through the dry seabed to safety. As they reached the other side, the pursuing Egyptian army was swallowed by the returning waters, leading to their ultimate defeat. God's strength, guidance, and presence were manifest, upholding His promise to protect and deliver the Israelites.

Moses' leadership and the miraculous crossing of the Red Sea exemplify the message of Isaiah 41:10. Despite facing seemingly impossible circumstances, Moses and the Israelites were reminded that God was with them. His strength and intervention were their source of courage and victory. Entrepreneurs can draw inspiration

47

from this story and understand that even in the face of overwhelming challenges, God's presence and empowerment can lead them through their difficulties to a place of triumph and success.

Entrepreneurial Insights: Bridging Isaiah 41:10 and Business

Fear Not: The verse begins by urging individuals not to fear. Entrepreneurs often encounter situations that evoke fear – whether it's the fear of failure, financial risk, or competition. Isaiah's message resonates by reminding entrepreneurs that they don't need to be paralyzed by fear; instead, they can approach challenges with faith and confidence.

God's Presence: "For I am with you." This phrase underscores the divine assurance of God's constant presence in the entrepreneurial journey. Entrepreneurs can find solace in knowing that they are not navigating the complexities of business alone; God is always with them, providing guidance, wisdom, and strength.

Divine Support: "I will strengthen you and help you." This declaration reinforces the idea that entrepreneurs don't have to rely solely on their own strengths and capabilities. God offers His strength and assistance, granting entrepreneurs the resilience needed to overcome obstacles and setbacks.

Upheld by God: "I will uphold you with my righteous right hand." This imagery symbolizes God's unwavering support. Just as a loving parent holds a child's hand, God is ready to lift entrepreneurs up, offering stability and protection in times of difficulty.

Courage Amidst Challenges: Entrepreneurs often face daunting challenges – financial uncertainties, market fluctuations, and fierce competition. Isaiah 41:10 encourages entrepreneurs to face these disheartening challenges with courage, trusting that God's presence and strength will help them persevere and succeed.

Confidence in Divine Plan: Knowing that God is in control provides a sense of calm and trust amid uncertainty. Entrepreneurs can move forward confidently, knowing that their journey is guided by a higher purpose and plan.

Overcoming Limitations: Entrepreneurs might feel inadequate or limited in their skills and resources. Isaiah 41:10 reminds them that with God's strength, they can transcend their limitations and achieve what might seem impossible.

Isaiah 41:10 offers a timeless message of hope and empowerment for everyday entrepreneurs. It encourages them to tackle challenges with confidence, knowing that God's presence, strength, and support are readily available. This verse inspires entrepreneurs to navigate their business journeys with faith, determination, and a deep sense of purpose, ultimately leading to breakthroughs and success beyond their own capabilities.

1. How can I practically integrate the assurance of God's presence and support, as mentioned in Isaiah 41:10, into my daily decision-making and problem-solving processes as an entrepreneur?

   _____

   _____

   _____

   _____

   _____

   _____

   _____

2. In what specific areas of my entrepreneurial journey do I find myself most prone to fear or anxiety, and how can I intentionally apply the "fear not" principle from Isaiah 41:10 to overcome these challenges?

   _____

   _____

   _____

   _____

_____

_____

_____

_____

3. In light of the promise of divine strength and assistance in Isaiah 41:10, how can I confidently balance my entrepreneurial drive and ambition with a willingness to rely on God's guidance and empowerment, especially when facing obstacles or uncertainties?

_____

_____

_____

_____

_____

_____

_____

Benefits: These questions encourage entrepreneurs to delve deeper into the implications of Isaiah 41:10 for their business endeavors, fostering self-awareness, actionable insights, and a stronger alignment with the verse's transformative principles.

Cultivating Growth: Insights to Propel Your Journey

Ladies and gentlemen, be open-minded for a tale that'll tickle your funny bone, tug at your heartstrings, and maybe even prompt a "hallelujah!" This story is about Bob, a quirky and ambitious entrepreneur with a penchant for witty one-liners and a knack for landing himself in sticky situations.

Meet Bob, the eternal optimist who decided to launch his dream business: a coffee shop that serves up caffeine and chuckles in equal measure. Armed with quirky décor and a hilarious menu, Bob's "Caffeine Comedy Café" was a hit among locals seeking a caffeine jolt and a good laugh.

But the entrepreneurial road wasn't all smooth sailing. One fateful morning, as Bob prepared his signature "Espresso Expressions," disaster struck. A leaky pipe turned his café into a mini swimming pool. Cue Bob's signature one-liner: "Well, guess we're diving into the espresso, folks!"

Amid the chaos, Bob's financial worries crept in like a persistent bad joke. It seemed like his entrepreneurial dreams were turning into a comedy of errors. Yet, amid his soggy café, Bob remembered Isaiah 41:10 – that divine promise of not being afraid.

With a newfound resolve, Bob rallied his staff and loyal customers to transform his café into a quirky underwater wonderland. Instead of despair, laughter echoed as customers waded through the café with waterproof boots, sharing jokes and making delightful memories. Bob stood at the center, realizing that God's presence was his ultimate punchline.

Word spread like wildfire about the "Splash and Sip" event at Caffeine Comedy Café. People flocked not just for coffee but for the contagious spirit of not letting obstacles dampen their spirits. Bob's café became a symbol of courage in the face of adversity.

As the waters receded and Bob's café returned to its dry state, he marveled at how his journey aligned with Isaiah 41:10. "Don't be dismayed, for I am your God," echoed in his mind. Bob embraced the truth that strength wasn't just about muscles; it was about a spirit that never backed down.

And so, the Caffeine Comedy Café flourished, not just as a coffee joint but as a living testament to overcoming fears and challenges with laughter and faith. As Bob stood in the doorway, watching customers leave with smiles and lighter hearts, he knew that amidst life's twists, turns, and leaky pipes, God's promise was the punchline that would keep him going.

So, my friends, let Bob's tale be a reminder that no matter how unpredictable the journey, the Creator's got your back. When life serves you leaks, turn them into laughter. And when things seem to go awry, fear not, for God's divine presence and strength will carry you through even the soggiest of situations.

Chapter 8: *Iron Sharpens Iron*

The Transformative Power of Entrepreneurial Connections

Proverbs 27:17 (NKJV): "As iron sharpens iron, so a man sharpens the countenance of his friend."

****

Principles in Action

The biblical story of David and Jonathan illustrates the principles found in Proverbs 27:17.

David and Jonathan's friendship is a profound example of how one person can sharpen another, just as iron sharpens iron. Jonathan, the son of King Saul, recognized David's potential and noble qualities. Despite his father's jealousy and opposition, Jonathan formed a deep bond with David, and their friendship grew stronger over time.

In 1 Samuel 18-20, we see how Jonathan's encouragement, loyalty, and wisdom sharpened David's character and decisions. Jonathan's selflessness and genuine concern for David's well-being supported David during times of adversity and uncertainty.

Their friendship reached its pinnacle when Jonathan warned David about Saul's intentions and helped him escape harm's way. Their connection was one of mutual respect, honesty, and support—qualities that contributed to the shaping of both their lives.

Connection to Proverbs 27:17

The story of David and Jonathan beautifully mirrors the principle in Proverbs 27:17. Just as iron sharpens iron, their friendship significantly sharpened each other's character, faith, and courage. Jonathan's encouragement and support during David's challenging journey demonstrated how one person can positively influence and elevate another.

This story teaches entrepreneurs that meaningful relationships are essential for personal growth and development. Carefully surrounding themselves with individuals who challenge, encourage, and inspire them can lead to sharpening their skills, perspectives, and decisions. Just as David and Jonathan benefited from each other's company, entrepreneurs can thrive by fostering connections that contribute to their growth and success.

The story of David and Jonathan underscores the truth of Proverbs 27:17 by showcasing the transformative power of authentic relationships. Entrepreneurs are encouraged to seek connections that sharpen their abilities and character, ultimately leading to a stronger and more impactful entrepreneurial journey.

The True Soul of Networking

In the dynamic landscape of entrepreneurship, the age-old wisdom of Proverbs 27:17 comes to life, revealing a profound truth: "As iron sharpens iron, so one person sharpens another." This timeless wisdom emphasizes the transformative power of relationships and collaboration, which resonates remarkably with the modern networking concept among entrepreneurs.

Just as iron becomes sharper when interacting with another piece of iron, entrepreneurs can experience a similar sharpening effect through intentional networking. By connecting with fellow entrepreneurs, they create a unique ecosystem of mutual growth, support, and innovation.

Entrepreneurs are often characterized by their unique vision, determination, and drive. However, the journey of entrepreneurship can be daunting and solitary. This is where the essence of Proverbs

27:17 comes to the forefront. Building and nurturing relationships with fellow entrepreneurs allows for the exchange of ideas, experiences, and expertise. Each interaction becomes an opportunity to gain fresh, advantageous perspectives, challenge assumptions, and refine strategies.

Networking fosters an environment where entrepreneurs share successes, failures, and lessons learned. Just as iron shapes iron through friction, entrepreneurs sharpen each other through constructive feedback and shared knowledge. Collaborative efforts often lead to innovative solutions and creative breakthroughs that wouldn't have been possible in isolation.

Moreover, the benefits of networking extend beyond immediate results. Cultivating relationships with diverse entrepreneurs exposes individuals to a variety of helpful industries, markets, and skill sets. It expands horizons, opens doors to new opportunities, and creates a network of potential partners, investors, and clients.

The entrepreneurial journey is characterized by continuous learning and adaptation. Networking serves as a living embodiment of Proverbs 27:17, driving personal and professional growth. Entrepreneurs can tap into the collective wisdom of their peers, equipping themselves with insights that lead to more informed decisions and, ultimately, greater success.

Networking amongst entrepreneurs is a powerful manifestation of the principles outlined in Proverbs 27:17. The process of connecting, collaborating, and learning from fellow entrepreneurs results in mutual sharpening and growth. By embracing the value of relationships, entrepreneurs create a community where the sum of collective knowledge is far greater than its individual parts. Through these connections, entrepreneurs find the support they need and a supportive platform for exponential growth, innovation, and lasting success.

Entrepreneurial Insights: Bridging Proverbs 27:17 and Business

Mutual Growth: Entrepreneurs can relate to the idea that just as iron becomes sharper when it interacts with another piece of iron, they, too, become better versions of themselves through interactions with fellow entrepreneurs. Engaging with peers allows for the exchange of helpful insights, experiences, and perspectives, fostering personal and professional growth.

Collective Wisdom: Entrepreneurs often face challenges and uncertainties unique to their endeavors. Connecting with other entrepreneurs offers access to a diverse range of knowledge and expertise. By pooling collective wisdom, entrepreneurs can make more informed decisions and navigate obstacles more effectively.

Innovation through Collaboration: Just as iron sharpens iron through friction, entrepreneurs can innovate and refine their ideas through constructive discussions and collaborative efforts. Networking encourages brainstorming, ideation, and problem-solving, leading to innovative solutions that may not have been possible in isolation.

Accountability and Feedback: Entrepreneurs can relate to the concept of sharpening through feedback. Interacting with peers provides opportunities for honest feedback and accountability. Constructive criticism from fellow entrepreneurs helps refine strategies, improve offerings, and enhance overall performance.

Expanding Horizons: Entrepreneurs often focus intensely on their own ventures, potentially missing out on broader industry trends or emerging opportunities. Networking exposes them to different perspectives, markets, and industries, expanding their horizons and enabling them to seize new possibilities.

Support and Encouragement: The entrepreneurial journey can be isolating and challenging. Relating to the idea of sharpening, entrepreneurs find support and encouragement from fellow entrepreneurs who understand their struggles and triumphs. This sense of community can provide the emotional sustenance needed to overcome hurdles.

Partnerships and Collaborations: Entrepreneurs can identify with the principle of one person sharpening another to achieve a common goal. Networking fosters the potential for partnerships, collaborations, and joint ventures, where entrepreneurs combine their strengths to achieve tremendous outcomes that may not have been attainable individually.

Proverbs 27:17 serves as a blueprint for the interdependent nature of entrepreneurship. Everyday entrepreneurs thrive when they seek connections with peers, recognizing that the sharpening process through interactions leads to growth, innovation, support, and collaborative success. By embracing the spirit of this verse, entrepreneurs enhance their journey and maximize their impact in the business world.

Harvesting Insights: Gold Mining for Business Growth

1. How can I actively seek out opportunities to engage with fellow entrepreneurs and industry peers in order to benefit from their diverse insights and experiences, aligning with the principle of mutual sharpening highlighted in Proverbs 27:17?

   _____

   _____

   _____

   _____

   _____

   _____

   _____

2. In what ways can I ensure that my interactions with other entrepreneurs are characterized by open-mindedness and a willingness to receive constructive feedback, recognizing that the sharpening process requires a receptive attitude for growth and improvement?

   _____

   _____

   _____

_____

_____

_____

_____

_____

3. What strategies can I implement to foster an environment of collaboration and shared learning within my network of fellow entrepreneurs, embracing the idea that collective wisdom and innovative ideas can emerge when one person sharpens another, as exemplified by Proverbs 27:17?

_____

_____

_____

_____

_____

_____

_____

Benefits: These questions encourage entrepreneurs to reflect on their approach to networking and collaboration, their receptiveness to feedback, and the proactive efforts they can undertake to create an environment where the principles of Proverbs 27:17 can thrive.

Cultivating Growth: Insights to Propel Your Journey

Ladies and gentlemen, let's explore. Can you imagine a bustling marketplace where the aroma of roasted chestnuts dances with the sounds of merchants haggling? In this vibrant scene, let me introduce you to two characters who, unbeknownst to them, were about to embody the very essence of Proverbs 27:17.

Meet Max and Leo, two eccentric entrepreneurs with wildly distinct ideas. Max was the inventor, a whiz with gadgets and gizmos. On the other hand, Leo was a wordsmith, penning eloquent prose that danced off the page. Their paths crossed one sunny day as they both set up shop side by side.

Now, Max thought his inventions were the bee's knees, but his contraptions seemed to malfunction just as often as they were amazed. With a touch of sarcasm, Leo quipped that Max's gadgets were "one switch away from becoming abstract art." Max laughed and retorted that Leo's words were just ink blots on parchment.

As time went on, their friendly banter turned into heated debates. Max claimed that innovation trumped eloquence any day, while Leo countered that words could create magic that rivaled any invention. Their disagreements echoed through the marketplace, capturing the attention of onlookers.

One day, a traveling sage named Seraphina heard their spirited discussions and decided to intervene. With a sly smile, she invited Max and Leo to a challenge. She told them about the famed "Enigma Cave" atop a nearby hill—an ancient riddle locked behind a stone door. Whoever solved it would win a treasure beyond measure.

Driven by their competitive spirits, Max and Leo accepted the challenge. As they scaled the hill, the weight of the riddle grew heavier with every step. When they reached the stone door, Seraphina whispered, "The answer lies in unity, not rivalry."

The riddle on the door read, "What's stronger than steel, yet softer than a sigh? It's built by two minds that can soar high."

Max scratched his head, Leo tapped his chin, and then, like a comedic duet, they blurted out in unison, "Iron sharpens iron!" The stone door swung open, revealing a treasure chest filled with laughter. Seraphina smiled knowingly and disappeared into the wind.

As Max and Leo shared a chuckle, they realized the profound truth behind the riddle. In their rivalry, they had sharpened each other's minds, turning debates into discussions, and arguments into a collaborative search for wisdom. They decided to pool their skills, creating gadgets that told stories, and stories that brought inventions to life.

From that day forward, their joint ventures thrived, and the marketplace buzzed with excitement over their imaginative creations. Their connection showed everyone that the collision of ideas, even if they seemed as different as night and day, could spark brilliance and camaraderie.

So, my friends, remember Max and Leo whenever you engage in spirited debates. For in the clash of thoughts and the clash of words, remember that it's not about who's right or wrong. It's about the magic that happens when two minds collide, shaping each other into sharper, wittier, and more creative versions of themselves. Just as iron sharpens iron, so do friends and fellow entrepreneurs sharpen each other and, in their unity, find treasure beyond measure.

Chapter 9: *From Ashes to Abundance*

Job's Tale of Restoration and Blessing

Job 42:12 (NKJV): "Now the Lord blessed the latter days of Job more than his beginning; for he had fourteen thousand sheep, six thousand camels, one thousand yoke of oxen, and one thousand female donkeys."

****

Principles in Action

The biblical story of Job illustrates the principles found in Job 42:12.

The story of Job is one of unwavering faith and eventual restoration. Job, a righteous man, faced immense suffering, losing his wealth, family, and health due to a series of trials. Despite his hardships, he remained faithful to God and questioned why he was enduring such adversity.

In the latter part of the story, after enduring his trials and maintaining his faith, God restored Job's fortunes. He received twice the wealth he had before—fourteen thousand sheep, six thousand camels, a thousand yoke of oxen, and a thousand donkeys. Job's faithfulness was recognized, and he experienced a profound blessing in the latter part of his life.

Connection to Job 42:12

Job's story beautifully aligns with the promise in Job 42:12. His life exemplified the concept of God's restoration and blessings after enduring trials. The latter part of Job's life was more prosperous than the former, showcasing God's faithfulness and the rewards of steadfast faith.

For entrepreneurs, Job's story highlights the potential for restoration and blessing after facing challenges and setbacks. Just as Job's faith was tested and ultimately rewarded, entrepreneurs can draw inspiration to persevere in the face of difficulties, knowing that there may be blessings awaiting them on the other side.

Entrepreneurs can find solace in Job's story by recognizing that their faith and endurance can lead to a season of restoration and growth. Just as Job's fortunes supernaturally turned around, entrepreneurs who remain committed to their vision and maintain their faith can experience renewed success, even after trial periods.

The story of Job illustrates the truth of Job 42:12 by demonstrating the principle of restoration and blessing after adversity. Entrepreneurs are encouraged to hold onto their faith, knowing that God's timing and providence can lead to blessings beyond their imagination, transforming the latter part of their journey into one of prosperity and fulfillment.

Entrepreneurial Insights: Bridging Job 42:12 and Business

Perseverance Through Adversity: Just as Job experienced profound trials and suffering, entrepreneurs often face daunting challenges and setbacks in their ventures. The story of Job reminds entrepreneurs that despite hardships, maintaining faith, resilience, and determination can lead to eventual restoration and blessings.

Renewed Vision and Growth: Entrepreneurs may encounter periods of difficulty where their vision seems obscured. Job's story emphasizes that such testing times can ultimately pave the divine way for renewed vision and growth. Entrepreneurs who navigate challenges with unwavering faith can emerge with a clearer sense of purpose and stronger determination.

Faith Amid Uncertainty: Job's unwavering faith amid his trials offers a powerful lesson for entrepreneurs navigating uncertainty. Just as Job remained faithful to God despite not understanding his circumstances, entrepreneurs can find solace in trusting the bigger picture and maintaining faith during times of ambiguity.

Blessings Beyond Imagination: Marked by restoration and increased blessings, the latter part of Job's story resonates with entrepreneurs who persevere through difficult seasons. This narrative underscores the idea that faithful endurance can lead to unexpected blessings and abundance, inspiring entrepreneurs to continue their journey with hope.

Reward for Steadfastness: Job's story showcases the principle that steadfastness in the face of adversity can lead to eventual rewards. Similarly, entrepreneurs who persist in pursuing their goals, even when faced with obstacles, can find reassurance that their dedication and perseverance will eventually yield positive outcomes.

Lessons in Humility: Job's humility and acknowledgment of God's sovereignty in his trials offer entrepreneurs a perspective on humility during challenges. Entrepreneurs can learn to approach difficulties with humility, humbly seeking lessons and growth even in the face of adversity.

Narrative of Transformation: The transformation from Job's initial suffering to his later abundance reflects the entrepreneurial journey's potential for transformation. Entrepreneurs can draw parallels, understanding that their challenges and perseverance can lead to personal growth and business success over time.

Job 42:12 serves as an encouraging beacon of hope and inspiration for everyday entrepreneurs. It encourages them to persevere through challenges, maintain faith in the face of uncertainty, and trust that their efforts and dedication will eventually lead to blessings and restoration beyond their expectations. Just as Job's story offers a testament of renewal and abundance, entrepreneurs can find encouragement to navigate their own journeys with faith, resilience, and the belief in future rewards.

1. How can I apply Job's example of maintaining unwavering faith and resilience during challenging times to my own entrepreneurial journey, and how might this mindset contribute to potential restoration and blessings in the long run?

    _____

    _____

    _____

    _____

    _____

    _____

    _____

2. In what ways can I embrace the lessons of humility and trust in God's providence that Job's story offers, particularly when facing setbacks or uncertainties in my business endeavors?

    _____

    _____

    _____

    _____

_____

_____

_____

_____

3. Considering the transformative journey from suffering to
    abundance in Job's story, how can I strategically navigate
    challenges and adversity with the understanding that they
    could potentially lead to renewed vision, growth, and
    unexpected blessings for my business?

    _____

    _____

    _____

    _____

    _____

    _____

    _____

Benefits: These questions encourage entrepreneurs to reflect on
the insights and principles found in Job 42:12, inviting them to apply

these lessons to their own entrepreneurial experiences and derive actionable strategies for navigating challenges and pursuing success.

Cultivating Growth: Insights to Propel Your Journey

Ladies and gentlemen, pay keen attention because I've got a tale that's about to unravel right before your very minds! Imagine a land where the sunsets painted the sky with hues of fire, and the wind whispered secrets to the trees. In this captivating landscape, let me introduce you to a character who's about to take us on a rollercoaster of emotions – the one and only Job.

Our story starts with Job, a man known for his prosperity and integrity. This guy had it all – camels, sheep, the fanciest donkeys you've ever seen. But let's not forget his seven sons and three daughters, each more beautiful than the last. You could say Job was living the dream, or so he thought.

Now, let's throw a twist into the mix. Satan – yep, that guy – he walks up to the heavens' gate like he's got VIP access. God's all, "What are you up to, Satan?" Satan replies, "Just wandering around, you know, chilling." But God knows better and tells Satan about Job, a man who's pretty much got his act together. Satan, being the cheeky guy he is, challenges Job's loyalty, saying he's only faithful because of all the good stuff he's got.

In a divine plot twist, God gives Satan permission to mess with Job's life but not lay a finger on him. And oh boy, does Satan take the challenge and run with it. Job's life crumbles like a cookie that's been dunked in hot cocoa for too long. His wealth vanishes, his kids meet an unfortunate end, and to top it off, he's covered in painful sores. Job's life takes a nosedive so epic it could rival a Hollywood blockbuster.

Job's friends arrive on the scene. They offer advice like a self-help book gone wrong, telling him he must've done something to deserve this misery. But Job, oh Job, he ain't having it. He's confused, frustrated, and downright ticked off at God. He's not gonna take this lying down.

Job demands an audience with the Creator himself. He wants answers, and he wants them now. He asks God the big questions, like "Why?" and "What's the meaning of all this?" And God? Well, let's just say He doesn't give Job the answers he expects. Instead, He takes Job on a cosmic journey, reminding him of His unfathomable power and wisdom.

Job humbles himself before God, realizing that there are deep mysteries beyond his understanding. He repents for his boldness and lack of knowledge, admitting that he spoke without truly comprehending the grand scheme of things.

God's not mad at Job. He's impressed by his honesty and humility. God restores Job's fortunes, blessing him with even more than he had before. Tested in the fires of suffering, Job's faith shines even brighter in the light of restoration.

So, dear friends, what can we learn from this epic tale? It's not just about Job's losses or his restoration. It's about the questions we ask when life throws us curveballs, the wrestling with our beliefs, and the journey from doubt to deeper understanding. Job 42:12 teaches us that through life's twists and turns, through our questions and uncertainties, there's a greater purpose at play. In the midst of it all, our faith can be refined, and blessings beyond our wildest dreams can be waiting on the other side.

Chapter 10: *Sow, Reap, Overflow*

Embracing Abundance through Generosity

Luke 6:38: "Give, and it will be given to you: good measure, pressed down, shaken together, and running over will be put into your bosom. For with the same measure that you use, it will be measured back to you."

****

Principles in Action

The Parable of the Good Samaritan, found in Luke 10:25-37, illustrates the principles highlighted in Luke 6:38.

In the Parable of the Good Samaritan, Jesus tells the story of a man who was attacked by robbers while traveling from Jerusalem to Jericho. The man is left wounded and half-dead on the roadside. A priest and a Levite pass by without offering help, but a Samaritan—a group despised by the Jews—stops to assist.

The Samaritan tends to the wounded man's wounds, takes him to an inn, and ensures he receives care. He even pays for the man's lodging and promises to cover any additional expenses upon his return.

Connection to Luke 6:38

The Parable of the Good Samaritan beautifully aligns with Luke 6:38's teachings on giving and generosity. In the parable, the Samaritan displays extraordinary generosity by going above and beyond to help a stranger in need. He doesn't hold back in offering his time, resources, and compassion to someone who cannot repay him.

The Parable of the Good Samaritan exemplifies the teachings of Luke 6:38 by showcasing the profound impact of selfless generosity. Entrepreneurs can learn a valuable lesson from this story and apply its lessons to their business and personal lives, reaping the rewards of abundance that come from giving freely and generously. Just as the Samaritan gives without expecting anything in return, the verse encourages individuals and entrepreneurs to give with a heart that overflows bountifully and immensely with kindness and abundance.

Entrepreneurial Insights: Bridging Luke 6:38 and Business

Building Strong Relationships: In the world of entrepreneurship, relationships are vital. The principle of "pressed down, shaken together, and running over" encourages entrepreneurs to invest in building meaningful connections. By giving generously in terms of trust, value, and empathy, entrepreneurs can foster stronger and more fruitful relationships.

Law of Reciprocity: Entrepreneurs can relate to the concept that the measure they give will be the measure they receive. Just as they invest effort, time, and resources into their business, Luke 6:38 encourages them to also invest in the well-being of their customers, employees, and communities. This reciprocal dynamic fosters loyalty, a positive reputation, and sustainable growth.

Creating Value: Entrepreneurs understand that success comes from creating value for others. Luke 6:38 encourages them to focus on providing exceptional value beyond what's expected. By exceeding customer expectations and enriching the lives of those they serve, entrepreneurs foster a loyal customer base and a positive reputation.

Community Impact: Entrepreneurs are part of larger communities. The verse's message of giving aligns with their potential to contribute positively to society. By engaging in philanthropy, supporting local initiatives, and addressing social needs, entrepreneurs can make a meaningful impact and earn the respect of their communities.

Rooted in the unwavering truth of 1 Corinthians 15:58, let us stand firm, knowing that our labor for the greater good is never in vain. As we continually pour our energy into selfless acts that support our community and uplift the hearts and spirits of those we've been called to serve, we're sowing seeds of kindness and generosity. Remember Luke 6:38; it's a promise that the measure we give will be returned, pressed down, shaken together, and running over. So, let's be steadfast and unmovable, knowing that our efforts create ripples of positive infectious change, not just for ourselves but for everyone we touch.

Planting Seeds for Future Growth: Just as farmers sow seeds in anticipation of a harvest, entrepreneurs can understand that their acts of giving and kindness plant seeds for future growth. Positive actions and contributions today can lead to long-term benefits, opportunities, and connections.

Abundance Mindset: Entrepreneurs often strive for success and abundance. Luke 6:38 reinforces the idea that a mindset of generosity and giving leads to an abundance of opportunities, connections, and even financial rewards. By freely sharing knowledge, resources, and support, entrepreneurs attract positivity and amplify their impact.

Differentiating from Competition: In competitive markets, entrepreneurs who go the extra mile and give generously can stand out from the crowd. Going beyond the expected, providing exceptional customer service, and demonstrating genuine care can set a business apart and attract loyal customers.

Luke 6:38 provides a guiding principle for everyday entrepreneurs, reminding and admonishing them that the energy they invest in giving, creating value, and positively impacting others will return to them in ways that surpass their expectations. By embodying an attitude of generosity, entrepreneurs can cultivate lasting success, meaningful relationships, and a legacy of positive influence.

1. How can I strategically incorporate an attitude of generosity and value creation into my business practices, not only for immediate gains but also with a long-term perspective of building lasting customer loyalty and positive relationships?

    _____

    _____

    _____

    _____

    _____

    _____

2. In what ways can I measure and assess the impact of my giving and value-driven efforts on various aspects of my business, such as customer retention, brand reputation, and overall growth?

    _____

    _____

    _____

_____

_____

_____

_____

3. Am I open to exploring collaborative opportunities and
    sharing insights with others in my industry, understanding
    that such knowledge exchanges can lead to innovative ideas
    and solutions, aligning with the principle of receiving in
    abundance, as stated in Luke 6:38?

    _____

    _____

    _____

    _____

    _____

    _____

    _____

Benefits: These questions encourage entrepreneurs to delve
deeper into the application of Luke 6:38's principles within their
business strategies. They prompt reflection on how giving, value

creation, and collaborative efforts can contribute to long-term success, customer satisfaction, and the overall impact of their ventures.

Cultivating Growth: Insights to Propel Your Journey

Ladies and gentlemen, brace yourselves for a story that's about to take your mind on a wild ride, like a rollercoaster of wisdom! Imagine a little village where chickens ruled the roost and the local bakery's aroma competed with the sunsets for attention. In this captivating village, let me introduce you to a character who's about to show us what it means to give like you're pouring from an endless jug – let's call him Sam, the Baker.

Sam's bakery was the talk of the town. People from neighboring villages would line up just to get a whiff of his freshly baked bread. But Sam wasn't just known for his delicious treats; he had a reputation for his heart of gold. He'd throw in an extra loaf for the elderly widow down the street and offer free pastries to kids who looked like they could use a sweet pick-me-up. His generosity was as warm as his oven.

One fine day, a traveling circus rolled into town. Acrobats flipped, clowns honked, and the ringmaster shouted like his voice was on fire. But amidst the dazzle, the circus was struggling to feed its performers. Sam, with his heart of gold and his bakery full of delights, couldn't just stand by. He whipped up baskets upon baskets of goodies and marched straight to the circus grounds.

As Sam walked in with his trays of treats, the circus performers stared in disbelief. But one performer, a trapeze artist named Elena, looked at Sam like he'd just given her the moon on a silver platter. She walked up to him, her eyes glistening, and thanked him like he'd performed a miracle. The other performers joined in, sharing stories of their hardships on the road.

Moved by their gratitude, Sam did the unexpected. He announced that his bakery would provide free treats for the circus every week they were in town. The circus performers erupted in cheers, and Elena gave Sam a hug that felt like gratitude wrapped in warmth.

Word spread like wildfire through the village about Sam's act of kindness. People flocked to his bakery not just for his pastries, but because they wanted to support someone who believed in giving abundantly. Sam's bakery became a hub of laughter, sharing, and community.

As the circus bid farewell to the village, Elena handed Sam a small trinket – a silver spoon with the words "Luke 6:38" engraved on it. Sam was puzzled and asked what it meant. Elena explained that it was a verse from the Good Book about giving and receiving. She told Sam that his generosity had sparked a cycle of kindness that would ripple through the village and beyond.

So, my friends, what do we learn from Sam the Baker's tale? Luke 6:38 isn't just about financial transactions; it's about the heart and soul you put into your giving. Sam's story teaches us that when you give like there's no end to your abundance, you create a world where generosity is currency and kindness is a feast. And remember, when you pour out love and kindness like Sam did, life serves up rewards that are sweeter than the finest pastry.

Chapter 11: *Divine Blueprint*

Unveiling the Prayer of Abundance and Authority

Matthew 6:9-13 (NKJV): "Our Father in heaven, Hallowed be Your name. Your kingdom come. Your will be done, on earth as it is in heaven. Give us this day our daily bread. And forgive us our debts, as we forgive our debtors. And do not lead us into temptation but deliver us from the evil one. For Yours is the kingdom and the power and the glory forever. Amen."

****

Principles in Action

The biblical story that perfectly illustrates Matthew 6:9-13 is the account of Jesus teaching his disciples how to pray, commonly known as the Lord's Prayer. In this passage, Jesus provides a template for a sincere and meaningful prayer that encompasses various aspects of a believer's relationship with God.

During one of his teachings, Jesus' disciples approached him, seeking guidance on how to pray effectively. They had observed how Jesus communicated with God and desired to have a similar connection. In response, Jesus shared what is now known as the Lord's Prayer, a model prayer that encapsulates the essence of a believer's relationship with their Heavenly Father.

Jesus began by addressing God as "Our Father in heaven." This simple yet profound phrase highlighted the intimate and familial nature of their relationship with God. It demonstrated that they could approach Him with the same reverence and trust as a child approaching their loving father.

As Jesus continued, he emphasized the sanctity of God's name and expressed the desire for God's kingdom to come and His will to be done on earth as it is in heaven. This portion of the prayer demonstrated the disciples' recognition of God's sovereignty and their submission to His divine plan.

The prayer also included a request for daily sustenance, acknowledging their dependence on God for their needs. By asking for "daily bread," the disciples expressed their trust in God's provision and acknowledged His role as the ultimate provider.

Forgiveness was another significant aspect of the prayer. Jesus taught them to seek God's forgiveness for their shortcomings while committing to forgiving others. This highlighted the importance of grace, mercy, and reconciliation within their relationships.

The prayer concluded with a plea for protection from temptation and deliverance from evil. By acknowledging their vulnerability to temptation and seeking God's guidance and strength to overcome it, the disciples demonstrated their reliance on God's power to navigate challenges.

In this illustrative story, Jesus' teaching of the Lord's Prayer showcases how Matthew 6:9-13 provides a comprehensive framework for a genuine and purposeful dialogue with God. It encapsulates themes of reverence, submission, dependence, forgiveness, and spiritual warfare, serving as a blueprint for believers to approach God with humility, faith, and confidence.

Entrepreneurial Insights: Bridging Matthew 6:9-13 and Business

Also known as the Lord's Prayer, Matthew 6:9-13 holds deep relevance for everyday entrepreneurs as it offers profound insights into their mindset, approach to challenges, and overall journey. Let's explore how this prayer resonates with the experiences of entrepreneurs:

Acknowledging Dependence: The prayer's opening words, "Our Father in heaven," underline believers' intimate relationship with God. Likewise, entrepreneurs can recognize their dependence on a higher power or greater purpose. This acknowledgment can inspire humility, grounding them amid the ups and downs of business ventures.

Alignment with Purpose: Entrepreneurs often wrestle with aligning their personal ambitions with a higher purpose. Just as the prayer seeks for God's will to be done, entrepreneurs can strive to align their business goals with a sense of purpose that goes beyond profit, fostering positive impact and meaningful contributions.

Daily Provision: Much like the prayer's request for "daily bread," entrepreneurs must manage daily operational challenges, ensuring the sustenance of their business. Trusting in God's provision while putting in diligent effort mirrors the entrepreneurial balance between faith and action.

Forgiveness and Relationships: In the prayer's plea for forgiveness and commitment to forgive, there's a lesson for entrepreneurs about the importance of maintaining healthy relationships. Business interactions can sometimes lead to conflicts, but a spirit of forgiveness and reconciliation can foster resilience and collaboration.

Overcoming Temptations: The line "lead us not into temptation but deliver us from evil" resonates with the entrepreneurial struggle against compromising values for short-term gains. This teaches entrepreneurs to make ethical decisions, even in the face of challenges, for the long-term sustainability of their ventures.

Guidance and Wisdom: Entrepreneurs often face uncertainty and difficult decisions. By seeking guidance from God, they can access divine wisdom to make informed choices, navigate complexities, and cultivate innovative solutions to problems.

Eternal Perspective: The Lord's Prayer points to a perspective beyond the immediate, urging believers to focus on eternal matters. Entrepreneurs, too, can look beyond the temporal achievements, placing value on lasting legacies, positive impact, and contributing to a greater good.

Courage in Trials: The prayer's essence of incessantly seeking God's strength encourages entrepreneurs to face adversity with courage. By understanding that challenges are opportunities for growth and learning, entrepreneurs can develop resilience and an unwavering spirit.

In true essence, Matthew 6:9-13 speaks to the heart of an entrepreneur's journey – the alignment of their endeavors with a higher purpose, the balance between faith and action, the importance of ethical decision-making, and the cultivation of qualities that lead to long-term success. It reminds entrepreneurs that, just like in prayer, a harmonious blend of trust, effort, wisdom, and resilience is key to navigating the complexities of the business world.

1. How can you incorporate the principles outlined in the Lord's Prayer (Matthew 6:9-13) into your entrepreneurial journey to cultivate a more profound sense of purpose and alignment with God's will?

   _____

   _____

   _____

   _____

   _____

   _____

   _____

   _____

2. In what ways does the concept of seeking "daily bread" in the Lord's Prayer relate to your business's financial and resource needs? How can you properly balance your proactive efforts with a genuine trust in God's provision?

   _____

   _____

   _____

   _____

_____

_____

_____

_____

3. The Lord's Prayer emphasizes forgiveness and reconciliation. How can you apply this principle to your interactions within the business world, including with partners, colleagues, and competitors? How might fostering an environment of forgiveness impact your business relationships and overall success?

_____

_____

_____

_____

_____

_____

_____

_____

Benefits: These questions provide a framework for entrepreneurs to evaluate their business practices and embark on a journey of holistic growth, ethical leadership, and meaningful impact by integrating spiritual principles into their entrepreneurial pursuits.

Cultivating Growth: Insights to Propel Your Journey

Ladies and gentlemen, brace yourselves and learn from this tale that'll make you chuckle, ponder, and find wisdom in unexpected places. Picture this: a bustling coffee shop, a self-assured barista named Lucy, and a divine lesson hidden in a cup of joe.

Meet Lucy, the coffee queen with a knack for whipping up the perfect brew and serving sass with a smile. Amid the hum of espresso machines and clinking cups, Lucy's coffee shop was a hub of caffeine-fueled camaraderie.

One fine day, a customer named Jack walked in, his face clouded with worries. As Lucy poured his cup, she noticed the weight on his shoulders. That's when she decided to share a lesson, straight from Matthew 6:9-13, with her unique brand of wisdom.

With a glint in her eye, Lucy handed Jack his coffee and said, "You know, in the prayer Jesus taught, there's a line that goes 'give us this day our daily bread.' Now, imagine if we treated life like a cup of coffee. Just like you trust me to serve you the perfect cup, you can trust God to provide for your needs."

Jack chuckled, intrigued by the coffee-shop theology. Lucy continued, "And when it says 'forgive us our debts as we forgive our debtors,' it's like stirring in sugar – the bitterness fades when you choose forgiveness. You sweeten your life."

Jack leaned in, captivated by Lucy's unconventional wisdom. She winked and said, "Now, when you ask not to be led into temptation but delivered from evil, it's like avoiding the stale coffee that's lost its flavor. Seek goodness, and you'll always sip from the cup of blessings."

As Jack left the coffee shop with a newfound bounce in his step, he realized that Matthew 6:9-13 was more than just words; it was a roadmap for life's rich brew. Lucy's coffee-shop parable had clearly shown him that faith, forgiveness, and a dash of divine guidance could infuse life with wonderful flavor beyond measure.

And so, every time Jack sipped his coffee, he remembered the lessons hidden in every verse. Just as Lucy had served him a cup of insight, he understood that life's greatest treasures could be found when we let God's insightful wisdom pour into our hearts.

So, my friends, as you savor your morning brew or tackle the day's challenges, let Lucy's tale remind you that wisdom can be found in the most unexpected places – even in a cup of coffee. Just like the prayer Jesus taught, let your life be a blend of trust, forgiveness, and divine guidance, creating a perfect brew of purpose and joy.

Chapter 12: *Sustenance in the Wilderness*

Unveiling Miracles of Provision

I Kings 17:8-16 (NKJV): "Then the word of the Lord came to him, saying, Arise, go to Zarephath, which belongs to Sidon, and dwell there. See, I have commanded a widow there to provide for you.' So, he arose and went to Zarephath. And when he came to the gate of the city, indeed a widow was there gathering sticks. And he called to her and said, 'Please bring me a little water in a cup, that I may drink.' And as she was going to get it, he called to her and said, 'Please bring me a morsel of bread in your hand.'

So, she said, 'As the Lord your God lives, I do not have bread, only a handful of flour in a bin, and a little oil in a jar; and see, I am gathering a couple of sticks that I may go in and prepare it for myself and my son, that we may eat it, and die.'

And Elijah said to her, 'Do not fear; go and do as you have said, but make me a small cake from it first, and bring it to me; and afterward make some for yourself and your son. For thus says the Lord God of Israel: 'The bin of flour shall not be used up, nor shall the jar of oil run dry, until the day the Lord sends rain on the earth.'

So, she went away and did according to the word of Elijah; and she and he and her household ate for many days. The bin of flour was not used up, nor did the jar of oil run dry, according to the word of the Lord which He spoke by Elijah."

****

Principles in Action

I Kings 17:8-16 narrates the story of Elijah and the widow of Zarephath. In this story, Elijah, a prophet, is directed by God to visit a widow in the town of Zarephath during a severe famine. The widow is gathering sticks to prepare a final meal for herself and her son before they succumb to hunger. Let's explore how this story illustrates I Kings 17:8-16 and its relevance to everyday entrepreneurs.

In the midst of a famine, Elijah is instructed by God to seek refuge with a widow in Zarephath. As he arrives at the town gate, he encounters the widow gathering sticks – a meager attempt to prepare a last meal for herself and her son.

Elijah approaches the widow and asks for a drink of water and a piece of bread. Distraught and honest, the widow explains her dire circumstances – she has only a handful of flour and a bit of oil left. She plans to use them to prepare a final meal for her son and herself before facing inevitable starvation.

Elijah, acting upon God's guidance, encourages the widow to prepare a small cake of bread for him first, promising that her supplies will not run out until the famine ends. Despite her reservations, the widow's faith leads her to follow Elijah's instructions.

Remarkably, as the widow obeys Elijah's directive, her supplies of flour and oil do not diminish but continue to sustain her household, just as Elijah had promised. It becomes evident that God's provision defies the natural limitations of scarcity.

The widow and her son experience a miraculous abundance of sustenance, which carries them through the famine. Their trust in God's guidance and Elijah's words resulted in a continued source of nourishment when circumstances seemed hopeless.

As you can see, the story of Elijah and the widow of Zarephath illustrates the concept of divine provision and the rewards of faith and obedience. Entrepreneurs can draw inspiration from the widow's journey, finding parallels in their own entrepreneurial endeavors as they navigate challenges and seek solutions that surpass natural limitations.

Entrepreneurial Insights: Bridging I Kings 17:8-16 and Business

The story of Elijah and the widow of Zarephath in I Kings 17:8-16 holds profound relevance for everyday entrepreneurs, offering valuable insights into faith, resourcefulness, and the potential for miraculous breakthroughs. Here's how this biblical narrative relates to entrepreneurs' journeys:

Resource Management: Like the widow who had limited resources, entrepreneurs often face situations with constraints on finances, time, and opportunities. This story significantly teaches entrepreneurs the importance of wise resource management, making the most of what they have, and exploring unconventional and creative solutions to overcome scarcity even when circumstances seem dire.

Faith in Uncertainty: Even though it seemed counterintuitive, the widow's act of faith in following Elijah's instructions mirrors the leaps of faith that entrepreneurs take when making decisions amidst uncertainty. The story encourages entrepreneurs to trust their instincts, embrace calculated risks, and step into the unknown with faith.

Miraculous Breakthroughs: The widow's obedience resulted in a miraculous provision of sustenance. Entrepreneurs can find inspiration in this narrative, understanding that their commitment, determination, and faith can lead to unexpected breakthroughs and God-given opportunities that transcend conventional limitations.

Networking and Collaboration: Elijah's encounter with the widow showcases the power of connections. Similarly, entrepreneurs can benefit from building relationships, seeking mentorship, and collaborating with others in their industry. These interactions can open doors to unexpected support and opportunities.

Generosity and Empathy: Elijah's presence brought hope and sustenance to the widow's life. Entrepreneurs can learn the value of extending a helping hand to others and fostering connections that bring mutual benefit.

Positive Mindset: The widow's willingness to give, despite scarce resources, highlights the value of maintaining a positive mindset. Entrepreneurs can learn to approach challenges with an attitude of generosity and resilience, trusting that their actions can influence positive outcomes.

Impactful Decision-Making: Just as Elijah's guidance transformed the widow's circumstances, entrepreneurs can seek guidance from mentors, advisors, and even their inner intuition when making critical decisions. This practice can lead to impactful choices that bring about significant change.

Embracing the Unknown: The widow's initial doubt and eventual compliance illustrate the journey entrepreneurs often undergo when stepping out of their comfort zones. This story encourages entrepreneurs to face uncertainty with courage and to remain open to unexpected solutions.

Spirit of Innovation: Entrepreneurs thrive by thinking outside the box, just as the widow did when she followed Elijah's unconventional instructions. The story highlights the importance of innovation and adaptability when pursuing business goals.

The narrative of Elijah and the widow of Zarephath offers entrepreneurs a powerful lesson in faith, resourcefulness, and the potential for divine intervention. It reminds them that their journey is not solely guided by conventional wisdom but by their willingness to embrace challenges, trust in their decisions, and remain open to the miraculous possibilities that can shape their entrepreneurial path.

Harvesting Insights: Gold Mining for Business Growth

1. In the face of limited resources, how can you draw inspiration from the widow's creative approach to scarcity in I Kings 17:8-16 and apply similar resourcefulness to your entrepreneurial challenges to achieve greater outcomes?

    _____

    _____

    _____

    _____

    _____

    _____

2. The widow in the story demonstrated faith by following Elijah's unconventional instructions. How can you incorporate a similar faith-driven approach into your decision-making process, especially when navigating uncertain or challenging circumstances in your business?

    _____

    _____

_____

_____

_____

_____

_____

3. Despite her limited resources, the widow took a calculated
    risk by obeying Elijah's guidance. How can you assess and
    strike a balance between practical considerations and
    calculated risks in your entrepreneurial decisions, particularly
    when faced with unconventional solutions that could lead to
    breakthroughs?

    _____

    _____

    _____

    _____

    _____

    _____

    _____

Benefits: These questions encourage entrepreneurs to reflect on the story's themes of resourcefulness, faith, and calculated risk-taking, and apply these principles to their own entrepreneurial journey.

Cultivating Growth: Insights to Propel Your Journey

Ladies and gentlemen, get ready for a tale that'll show you how even a pot of flour can pack a lesson worth more than gold. It all starts in a quaint village named Flour Ville, where a curious entrepreneur named Eddie embarked on an unforgettable adventure.

Meet Eddie, the unpredictable and one-of-a-kind entrepreneur who believed that every challenge was just a business opportunity in disguise. Flour Ville was facing its worst famine in years, and Eddie saw this as his chance to shine, armed with his boundless optimism and a dash of eccentricity.

While strolling through the village one day, Eddie witnessed an unusual scene. A widow named Millie was outside her cottage, scraping together the last remnants of flour in her pot, a gloomy expression painted on her face. Eddie's curiosity was piqued – a gloomy customer meant a potential business venture!

With his infectious enthusiasm, Eddie approached Millie and asked, "Say, my friend, what's cooking? And why the long face?" Millie sighed and explained her dire situation – her last bit of flour and oil were meant for a final meal for her son and herself. Eddie's eyes twinkled, for he saw an opportunity to turn flour into fortune.

With a mischievous grin, Eddie proposed a deal. He convinced Millie to lend him a bit of flour and oil, assuring her that he had a brilliant plan that would make their bellies and pockets fuller than ever. Millie, intrigued by his audacity, agreed – partly out of curiosity and desperation.

Eddie swung into action, gathering the villagers, and hosting a grand baking competition. The catch? Each participant had to use Millie's meager flour and oil to create a delectable dish.

The villagers were skeptical, but Eddie's charm and vision were quite infectious. And so, the Flour Ville Bake-Off began!

As the bakers mixed, kneaded, and baked, magic happened. The villagers, driven by competition and camaraderie, transformed the scarce ingredients into a feast fit for royalty.

Eddie's audacious idea turned into a resounding success, proving that even amid scarcity, innovation could lead to abundance.

With bellies full and spirits high, the villagers cheered for Eddie's creative genius. The once-gloomy Millie couldn't believe her eyes – her meager ingredients had sparked a revolution of resourcefulness. And as Flour Ville savored the fruits of their labor, they learned a lesson that echoed through the ages – that even the tiniest bit of faith and innovation could turn scarcity into surplus.

So, my friends, as you journey through your entrepreneurial endeavors, remember Eddie and his Flour Ville tale. When faced with scarcity, let your audacious spirit rise, and your creative thinking shine.

Just like Eddie turned a pot of flour into a village feast, you, too, can transform challenges into opportunities that defy expectations and fill your entrepreneurial journey with flavors of success and laughter.

Chapter 13: *Masterpieces in Motion*

Unveiling Your Purposeful Creation

Ephesians 2:10 (NKJV): "For we are His workmanship, created in Christ Jesus for good works, which God prepared beforehand that we should walk in them."

****

Principles in Action

While there isn't a specific biblical story that directly illustrates Ephesians 2:10, which reads, "For we are God's masterpiece, created in Christ Jesus to do good works, which God prepared in advance for us to do," the Bible contains themes and narratives that align with this verse. One notable example is the story of Joseph in the Book of Genesis.

Joseph, the son of Jacob, experienced a series of trials and triumphs that ultimately led to a greater purpose. Despite facing betrayal, slavery, and imprisonment, Joseph's unwavering faith and resilience showcased how God's plan was at work in his life. His journey eventually led him to a position of authority in Egypt, where he played a crucial role in saving the region from famine and reuniting with his family.

While not a direct parallel, Joseph's story highlights themes of God's sovereignty, purpose, and the idea of being part of a greater plan. His experiences exemplify how individuals can be molded through challenges to fulfill a greater purpose, much like the message of Ephesians 2:10.

In your interpretation of Ephesians 2:10, you can draw inspiration from various stories in the Bible that emphasize how individuals are uniquely created and designed by God to fulfill specific roles and purposes, even if there isn't a perfect one-to-one match.

Entrepreneurial Insights: Bridging Ephesians 2:10 and Business

With its powerful declaration that "For we are God's masterpiece, created in Christ Jesus to do good works, which God prepared in advance for us to do," Ephesians 2:10 holds profound relevance for everyday entrepreneurs. Here's how this verse relates to their journey:

Uniqueness of Purpose: Just as every individual is God's masterpiece, every entrepreneur possesses a unique set of talents, skills, and experiences. Recognizing and embracing this uniqueness enables entrepreneurs to discover their purpose and contribute in ways that align with their strengths.

Divine Preparation: The verse emphasizes that God prepared good works in advance for us. In the entrepreneurial context, this speaks to the idea that opportunities and challenges are part of a bigger plan. Entrepreneurs can find solace in knowing that their journey is guided by a higher purpose.

Business as Ministry: Entrepreneurs can view their businesses as platforms to carry out the "good works" mentioned in the verse. By creating value, serving customers, and positively impacting their communities, entrepreneurs align their endeavors with their faith and make their businesses a form of ministry.

Resilience and Faith: Entrepreneurial journeys are often marked by challenges. Ephesians 2:10 encourages entrepreneurs to navigate these challenges with faith and resilience, trusting that their efforts are part of a larger tapestry that God is weaving.

Fulfillment and Contentment: Pursuing ventures that align with one's purpose brings a sense of fulfillment and contentment. Entrepreneurs who understand that they are part of God's design can find deeper satisfaction in their achievements, knowing that they are fulfilling their unique calling.

Legacy of Impact: Ephesians 2:10 encourages entrepreneurs to focus on leaving a legacy of positive impact. By using their businesses to do good works, entrepreneurs create a ripple effect that extends beyond profits, enriching lives and communities.

Ethical and Compassionate Practices: The verse reminds entrepreneurs that they are God's masterpiece, responsible for acting ethically and compassionately in their business dealings. This includes treating employees, customers, and partners with respect and fairness.

Balancing Ambition and Alignment: Entrepreneurs can align their ambitions with their divine purpose, ensuring that their pursuits are in harmony with their faith and values. This alignment provides a sense of direction and clarity amidst the complexities of entrepreneurship.

Overwhelmingly, Ephesians 2:10 encourages everyday entrepreneurs to view their journey as a canvas upon which they create meaningful business works, guided by purpose, integrity, and the assurance that they are part of a divine plan that transcends conventional success.

Harvesting Insights: Gold Mining for Business Growth

1. How can you reflect on your unique talents, skills, and experiences to uncover the entrepreneurial purpose that aligns with the idea that you are God's masterpiece, created for specific good works?

_____

_____

_____

_____

_____

_____

2. In what ways can you strategically integrate your faith into your business endeavors, ensuring that your entrepreneurial pursuits are in harmony with the concept of being created to do good works that were prepared in advance?

_____

_____

_____

_____

_____

_____

_____

_____

3. How can you evaluate your business's impact on customers, employees, and communities to ensure that your entrepreneurial actions resonate with the idea that you are part of a divine plan, passionately contributing positively to the lives of others?

_____

_____

_____

_____

_____

_____

_____

Benefits: These questions encourage entrepreneurs to critically reflect on their purpose, values, and impact, cautiously aligning their entrepreneurial journey with the principles highlighted in Ephesians 2:10.

Cultivating Growth: Insights to Propel Your Journey

Ladies and gentlemen, brace yourselves for a tale that'll tickle your intellect and stir your soul – a tale of a very peculiar inventor, a mysterious blueprint, and a revelation that even the most brilliant minds couldn't have concocted.

Meet Professor Quincy, an inventor with wild hair and an even wilder imagination. In the heart of Innovation City, Quincy's workshop was a whirlwind of gears, gadgets, and gizmos. He was known for his audacious ideas and eccentricities, but there was one thing he couldn't quite invent – a sense of purpose.

One fateful day, a mysterious blueprint appeared on Quincy's workbench. Curious and intrigued, he studied the blueprint's intricate design, which seemed to depict a device that didn't quite make sense to him. Determined to crack the code, Quincy embarked on a journey to bring this enigma to life.

Weeks turned into months as Quincy tinkered, toiled, and tinkered some more. His determination was unwavering, fueled by an unquenchable desire to unveil the purpose behind this peculiar blueprint. But the device refused to cooperate, defying Quincy's every attempt to bring it to fruition.

Exhausted and frustrated, Quincy found himself at a crossroads. He gazed at the incomplete device, feeling defeated and wondering if he was chasing a dream that was beyond his reach. In that moment of vulnerability, a voice echoed in his mind – "For you are God's masterpiece."

As Quincy pondered those words, a realization washed over him like a wave. He wasn't just an inventor; he was a masterpiece in the making, created with a purpose beyond gears and gadgets. He looked at the incomplete device with fresh eyes, seeing not just its physical components but the potential for impact it represented.

With newfound determination, Quincy shifted his perspective. He realized that the device's purpose wasn't solely to solve a mechanical puzzle but to create something that would improve lives, inspire innovation, and foster connections among people.

Quincy's journey of self-discovery led him to invent not just a device but a movement., Now a symbol of purpose and creativity, the completed device became a centerpiece in Innovation City. People from all walks of life gathered to marvel at Quincy's creation; everyone was inspired to uncover their own purpose and contribution.

From that day on, Quincy's workshop became a hub for purpose-driven innovation. Entrepreneurs, artists, and dreamers of all kinds flocked to him, seeking technical expertise and the wisdom to align their endeavors with their unique purpose, just as Ephesians 2:10 had illuminated for Quincy.

So, my friends, as you embark on your own journey of creation and discovery, remember Professor Quincy and his blueprint tale. Let your entrepreneurial pursuits be a testament to the truth that you are a masterpiece, designed for good works that extend beyond what meets the eye. And who knows, just like Quincy, you might not just invent a solution – you might just invent a revolution of purpose that transforms lives and shapes the world.

Chapter 14: *Never Fold*

Defiant Faith Amidst the Flames

Daniel 3:12 (NKJV): "But there are some Jews whom you have set over the affairs of the province of Babylon—Shadrach, Meshach and Abednego—who pay no attention to you, Your Majesty. They neither serve your gods nor worship the image of gold you have set up."

****

Principles in Action

While there isn't a specific biblical story that directly illustrates Daniel 3:12, which reads, "But there are some Jews whom you have set over the affairs of the province of Babylon—Shadrach, Meshach and Abednego—who pay no attention to you, Your Majesty. They neither serve your gods nor worship the image of gold you have set up." The story of Shadrach, Meshach, and Abednego in the fiery furnace aligns with the context of this verse.

The Story of Shadrach, Meshach, and Abednego: In the book of Daniel, King Nebuchadnezzar erected a massive golden statue and commanded everyone to bow down and worship it. However, Shadrach, Meshach, and Abednego, three Jewish officials, refused to bow to the statue as it contradicted their faith in God.

Their defiance of the king's order parallels the sentiment expressed in Daniel 3:12. The verse highlights that these individuals, whom Nebuchadnezzar had appointed to high positions, did not succumb to fear or compromise their faith. They stood firm and refused to fold to societal pressures, even in the face of severe consequences.

The story of Shadrach, Meshach, and Abednego demonstrates how their unwavering commitment to their faith and principles resulted in God's miraculous intervention, protecting them in the midst of the fiery furnace. This story illustrates the idea that it's possible to remain steadfast in one's beliefs and values, even when confronted with challenging situations – a theme that resonates with the sentiment expressed in Daniel 3:12.

Entrepreneurial Insights: Bridging Daniel 3:12 and Business

Unwavering Conviction: Just as Shadrach, Meshach, and Abednego remained resolute in their faith, entrepreneurs can draw inspiration to stand unwaveringly by their convictions and principles. In the face of business challenges or societal pressures, staying true to core values can lead to long-term success and respect.

Defying Conformity: Entrepreneurs often operate in a competitive landscape where there may be pressures to conform or compromise for short-term gains. Daniel 3:12 reminds them that staying true to their vision and values can set them apart, enabling them to make a lasting impact on their industry.

Leadership with Integrity: Shadrach, Meshach, and Abednego were entrusted with leadership positions. Similarly, entrepreneurs who uphold their integrity and prioritize ethical practices inspire trust and confidence among their team, clients, and stakeholders.

Risk-Taking for Beliefs: Just as the three refused to bow to the golden statue, entrepreneurs may need to take calculated risks to uphold their values and create positive change. This can involve challenging the status quo, introducing innovative ideas, and standing firm against unethical practices.

Courage in Adversity: Entrepreneurs often face challenges that test their resolve. Just as Shadrach, Meshach, and Abednego faced the fiery furnace, entrepreneurs can draw strength from their faith, principles, and inner courage to overcome seemingly insurmountable obstacles.

Divine Protection: The story illustrates that standing firm in one's beliefs can lead to divine intervention and protection. Entrepreneurs who, with faith, prioritize values often find that their resilience is rewarded through unexpected solutions and opportunities.

Inspiring Others: The actions of Shadrach, Meshach, and Abednego inspired not only their peers but generations to come. Similarly, entrepreneurs who remain unyielding in their convictions can inspire others to do the same and positively impact their community and industry.

In the world of entrepreneurship, Daniel 3:12 serves as a reminder that staying true to one's principles, even when faced with challenges or opposition, can lead to remarkable outcomes, personal growth, and the potential to create meaningful change.

1. How can I ensure that my business decisions and practices align with my core values, even in situations where external pressures may encourage compromise?

   _____

   _____

   _____

   _____

   _____

   _____

   _____

2. In what ways can I strike a balance between adhering to industry norms and introducing innovative approaches that reflect my unique vision and convictions?

   _____

   _____

   _____

   _____

   _____

_____

_____

_____

3. How can I lead by example to foster a work culture where my team members feel empowered to uphold their principles and maintain integrity, even when faced with discouraging challenges?

_____

_____

_____

_____

_____

_____

Benefits: These questions encourage entrepreneurs to critically reflect on the alignment of their actions with their values and how they can lead and inspire others to stand firm in their convictions, echoing the spirit of Daniel 3:12.

Cultivating Growth: Insights to Propel Your Journey

Ladies and gentlemen, pay keen attention to this life-changing tale. This is a tale of defiant courage, blazing fires, and a trio of entrepreneurs who refused to be burned by conformity.

Meet the city of Enterprise, a bustling metropolis where entrepreneurship reigned supreme. At the heart of it all were three entrepreneurs – Shadrach, Meshach, and Abednego. Renowned for their innovative ventures, these three weren't just business moguls; they were fire starters of creativity and change.

But trouble brewed when King Nebuchadnezzar introduced a gargantuan golden statue and decreed that everyone must bow to it. The city was ablaze with compliance, but not these three. Amid the crowd's bowing heads, they stood tall, their spines straighter than ever.

News of their defiance reached the king's ears like wildfire. He summoned the trio, his anger blazing hotter than the sun. "Are these allegations true?" he roared, pointing at the unyielding entrepreneurs. "You dare challenge my command?"

Shadrach, Meshach, and Abednego looked into the king's eyes, their resolve unwavering. "Your majesty," they replied, "we're no strangers to entrepreneurship. We've built our ventures on integrity, innovation, and values. Bowing to a statue is not a venture we're willing to undertake."

Nebuchadnezzar's rage intensified, and he ordered a fiery furnace to be heated seven times hotter than usual. But as the entrepreneurs faced the inferno, an unexpected spectacle unfolded. There, in the midst of the flames, walked a fourth figure – an otherworldly presence that shielded them from harm.

109

The sight astounded the king, and he summoned the trio from the furnace, now unscathed by the fire. "How is this possible?" he exclaimed, his fury transformed into awe. "Our faith and conviction in our entrepreneurial values protected us," they explained.

News of the entrepreneurs' fiery stand spread across Enterprise like wildfire. Their unwavering commitment to their principles ignited a movement, inspiring other business leaders to stand up against conformity and prioritize values, even in the face of adversity.

As the trio continued their entrepreneurial journey, they did more than just build businesses; they became fires of courage and innovation. Their city thrived not just economically but ethically, setting a new standard for the entrepreneurial landscape.

So, dear friends, as you tread the path of entrepreneurship, remember Shadrach, Meshach, and Abednego – the flames couldn't consume them because their values burned brighter. In your journey of creativity, innovation, and business, don't be afraid to stand tall against the fiery temptations of conformity. Be entrepreneurs who defy the norm and rise above the flames, for just like these three, you have a fourth presence – the spirit of unwavering principles – to protect and guide you to heights you've never imagined.

Dedication of Chapter 14

This chapter is inspired by and dedicated to the Founders of the Never Fold Movement. Cornelius Lewis (Blessed Story) and Daynuh Lewis (Mrs. Blessed). Never Fold Movement is an organization whose sole purpose is to give back to the community in various ways. As part of the Never Fold Movement, they feed and clothe those in need, have mentorship and entrepreneurship programs for inner city youth and those transitioning out of prison back into society. One of their biggest missions is sowing into world missions as well as being part of funding the end-time harvest.

Chapter 15: *Soul's Oasis*

Journey of Comfort and Renewal in Psalm 23

Psalm 23 (NKJV): "The Lord is my shepherd; I shall not want. He makes me to lie down in green pastures; He leads me beside the still waters. He restores my soul; He leads me in the paths of righteousness for His name's sake. Yea, though I walk through the valley of the shadow of death, I will fear no evil; For You are with me; Your rod and Your staff, they comfort me. You prepare a table before me in the presence of my enemies; You anoint my head with oil; My cup runs over. Surely goodness and mercy shall follow me all the days of my life; And I will dwell in the house of the Lord forever."

****

Principles in Action

The biblical story of Moses leading the Israelites through the wilderness, as told in the book of Exodus, beautifully illustrates the themes of Psalm 23.

In the story of Moses and the Israelites, the people of Israel are led by Moses through the harsh and challenging wilderness as they journey toward the Promised Land. Along the way, they face trials, uncertainties, and the need for sustenance.

The story of Moses and the Israelites is rich in lessons about faith, deliverance, leadership, and obedience. It highlights the Israelites' transformation from slavery to a journey of faith, guided by God's presence and provision.

Connection to Psalm 23

The Israelites' journey through the wilderness mirrors the experiences described in Psalm 23. Just as a shepherd guides and provides for his sheep, In his role as a leader, Moses guides and provides for the people of Israel as they navigate the challenges of the wilderness.

Entrepreneurial Insights: Bridging Psalm 23 and Business

Psalm 23 holds profound relevance for everyday entrepreneurs, offering them guidance and comfort amid their demanding journey:

Guidance and Protection: Just as a shepherd guides and protects their flock, Psalm 23 reminds entrepreneurs that they are not alone. It reassures them that a higher power is watching over them, providing guidance through challenges and protection from potential harm. Just as Moses led the Israelites through the wilderness, entrepreneurs can find solace in knowing that they are not alone in navigating difficulties.

Rest and Renewal: The imagery of "green pastures" and "still waters" encourages entrepreneurs to find moments of rest and rejuvenation amidst their busy schedules. Taking breaks, prioritizing self-care and renewal, and nurturing their well-being are vital for sustained productivity and creativity. The balance between striving and resting ensures sustained creativity, energy, and the ability to embrace the journey wholeheartedly.

Fear Management: The Israelites faced fear and uncertainty as they journeyed through unfamiliar territory. "Though I walk through the valley of the shadow of death, I will fear no evil." This line resonates with entrepreneurs who often encounter uncertainties and fears on their journey. It also echoes the courage they must embody in their pursuits. The entrepreneurial journey is rife with uncertainties, but cultivating fearlessness and unwavering faith empowers them to overcome obstacles. Psalm 23 teaches them to face challenges head-on with courage, trusting in their ability and knowing that fear can be overcome.

Divine Provision: The reference to a "table prepared in the presence of enemies" symbolizes abundance even in difficult circumstances. The Israelites' reliance on God for sustenance in the wilderness parallels entrepreneurs' need for resources and support in their ventures. For entrepreneurs, this signifies that resources and opportunities can arise even amidst challenges, and trusting in a higher power can lead to unexpected breakthroughs.

Long-Term Vision: The Israelites' journey had a larger purpose: reaching the Promised Land. Entrepreneurs can apply this by maintaining a long-term vision for their business, understanding that their business challenges contribute to their growth and ultimate success.

The journey isn't just about the present but also the Promised Land of their goals. Embrace each challenge and triumph as steps toward a purposeful destination, trusting that their path is leading them to greatness.

Guided Paths: Entrepreneurs often face decisions with no clear path forward. The verse "He leads me in paths of righteousness" emphasizes the importance of seeking guidance in decision-making. Entrepreneurs can trust that their choices are guided by divine wisdom.

Comfort in Times of Struggle: The promise of God's "rod and staff" brings comfort to entrepreneurs during moments of difficulty. This reassurance encourages them to persevere, knowing that challenges are temporary, and they can emerge stronger on the other side.

Optimism and Gratitude: Psalm 23's overall tone of gratitude encourages entrepreneurs to cultivate a positive mindset. Focusing on blessings, achievements, and the support around them fosters an optimistic outlook despite unforeseen challenges.

Embracing Community: The reference to "anointing my head with oil" and "my cup overflows" symbolizes abundant blessings. Entrepreneurs can interpret this as an encouragement to share their blessings, supporting their team, community, and those less fortunate.

In summary, Psalm 23 serves as a guiding light for everyday entrepreneurs, reminding them to navigate their journey with faith, courage, self-care, and gratitude. It underscores the importance of seeking divine guidance, finding rest amidst the chaos, and fostering a resilient spirit, ultimately leading to a more balanced and purposeful entrepreneurial life.

Harvesting Insights: Gold Mining for Business Growth

1. How can I practically implement the concept of finding "green pastures" and "still waters" in my entrepreneurial routine to ensure consistent rest and rejuvenation, leading to improved productivity and well-being?

   _____

   _____

   _____

   _____

   _____

   _____

   _____

   _____

2. In what ways can I apply the principle of fear management from Psalm 23 to address challenges and uncertainties in my business with courage and resilience, fostering an environment of innovation and growth?

   _____

   _____

   _____

   _____

_____

_____

_____

_____

3. Considering the idea of divine guidance in decision-making
    presented in Psalm 23, how can I integrate moments of
    reflection and seeking wisdom from a higher source into my
    entrepreneurial strategy to make more informed and
    purposeful choices?

_____

_____

_____

_____

_____

_____

Benefits: These questions encourage entrepreneurs to delve
deeper into the practical application of Psalm 23's wisdom within
their business endeavors. They prompt purposeful reflection on self-

care, courage, and decision-making, guiding entrepreneurs toward a more balanced and spiritually grounded approach to their entrepreneurial journey.

Cultivating Growth: Insights to Propel Your Journey

Ladies and gentlemen, let's critically observe this tale that'll make you think while keeping a smile firmly planted on your face. Let me introduce you to a character who's about to take us on a journey of faith, resilience, and a bit of sheep wrangling - let's call him Leo, the Shepherd.

Leo wasn't your ordinary shepherd; he was a bit of a joker, always ready with a quip and a hearty laugh. He tended to his flock of sheep with the kind of love that comes from a heart as vast as the open fields. One day, as Leo led his sheep to graze, he stumbled upon a narrow, winding path that led to a lush valley. It was almost like a secret haven, tucked away from the world's chaos.

Leo marveled at the serenity of the valley, its still waters reflecting the blue of the sky. His sheep also seemed to sense the calmness, as if they'd found their own piece of paradise. But Leo wasn't just there for a scenic picnic; he was there to teach us a lesson in the most Leo sort of way possible.

As Leo settled down under a tree, his sheep scattered around him, he began to recite Psalm 23. But here's the twist: Each verse was paired with one of Leo's humorous anecdotes. He mimicked the sheep getting stuck in thorns, comparing it to "lying down in green pastures" - because sheep can't resist a snack, even if it means getting prickled!

The climax arrived as Leo shared a story about a mischievous lamb that always wandered off. He spun this yarn as he recited, "He leads me beside still waters." The crowd chuckled, envisioning the lamb trying to outwit Leo, only to be gently guided back to safety.

The sheep listened, seemingly nodding in agreement with each comedic twist. As Leo wrapped up his unique rendition of Psalm 23, he emphasized how the verses reminded him of his flock's adventures. Yet, underneath the humor, he conveyed the deep sense of protection, guidance, and comfort that the words offered.

Leo's storytelling session had an unexpected impact. The laughter turned into contemplation, and the lesson he shared that day stuck with everyone who gathered. His unconventional approach to teaching Psalm 23 made it relatable, memorable, and applicable to their own lives.

And so, my friends, let's remember Leo, the Shepherd, and his whimsical wisdom. Psalm 23 isn't just a sequence of words; it's a roadmap for life's journey. Just like Leo led his sheep to the serene valley, this Psalm leads us to a place of faith, courage, and a deeper connection to the divine shepherd who divinely guides us through every twist, turn, and comedic sheep escapade on our unique entrepreneurial paths.

Conclusion

As you reach the conclusion of "Entrepreneurial Giants," you're not just closing a book—you're confidently stepping into a new paradigm of entrepreneurial wisdom and faith-infused success. This journey has been one of revelation and transformation, a voyage that ignites your spirit and equips you with the tools to conquer any business challenge.

Invaluable Nuggets and Key Takeaways

Faith as Your North Star: Throughout history, faith has been the cornerstone of greatness. David's audacity, Esther's pioneering spirit, and Paul's perseverance all stem from unwavering faith. Let their stories guide you as you navigate the entrepreneurial landscape.

Proactive Excellence: Embrace the spirit of diligence and proactive excellence. Proverbs 22:29 reminds us that our skills and efforts shape our destiny. Be the craftsman of your success, proactively chiseling away limitations and carving a path of distinction.

Unleash Limitless Strength: Like Paul, tap into the limitless strength that comes from embracing Christ's empowerment. Let your weaknesses become a canvas for divine intervention, transforming obstacles into stepping stones.

Stewardship and Abundance: Luke 16:10 teaches us the power of mastering the small to seize the grand. As you steward your resources, from time to talent, abundance will flow, and your impact will expand.

Embrace Risk with Courage: Like Ecclesiastes 11:6 suggests, seize the winds of opportunity. Face risk with courage, and your endeavors will propel you toward uncharted horizons of success.

Rise Strong with Faith: Isaiah 41:10 reassures that fear should not overpower you; rather, let faith guide your journey. Harness divine power to strategically overcome challenges and rise strong in the face of adversity.

Entrepreneurial Connections: Just as iron sharpens iron, seek and nurture relationships that elevate your entrepreneurial journey. Collaboration and unity will amplify your growth and impact.

Transformation Through Restoration: Experience the transformative power of restoration, much like Job did. From ashes to abundance, your trials can pave the way for a renewed and prosperous future.

Sow, Reap, Overflow: Luke 6:38 reminds us of the law of abundance. Embrace generosity in your actions and mindset, and watch your endeavors multiply beyond measure.

Blueprint for Prayerful Authority: Matthew 6:9-13 unveils a prayer that holds the blueprint for authority and abundance. Infuse your endeavors with prayer, aligning your intentions with divine guidance.

Miracles of Provision: I Kings 17:8-16 illustrates that miracles of provision await those who remain faithful. Trust that sustenance will flow into your journey, even in the wilderness.

Unveil Your Purposeful Creation: Ephesians 2:10 celebrates the masterpiece you are, designed for purposeful creation. Let this knowledge fuel your actions and decisions, knowing your potential is limitless.

Defiant Faith Amidst Flames: In the spirit of Daniel 3:12, never fold under adversity. Let your faith burn like an unquenchable fire, propelling you to greater heights.

Journey of Comfort and Renewal: Let Psalm 23 be your divine compass, reminding you that in the vast landscape of entrepreneurship, a shepherd's care guides, protects, and nourishes you. Embrace its teachings, for within its verses lie the secrets to navigating challenges with grace, creating a legacy rooted in faith, and finding peace amidst the entrepreneurial journey's breathtaking peaks and challenging valleys.

"Entrepreneurial Giants" isn't just a book—it's a catalyst for transformation. It's an invitation to unleash your entrepreneurial potential through biblical principles. As you close these pages, remember that every challenge is an opportunity, every setback a setup for a comeback.

This conclusion isn't the end; it's just the beginning of your journey toward supernatural entrepreneurial triumph. With each page, you've delved into a wellspring of wisdom that will fuel your actions, inspire your decisions, and amplify your impact. The dialogue between faith and business continues—prepare yourself for more.

Let these pages linger in your heart, constantly reminding you that the giants of the past stand as your companions in the present. Go forth with audacity, courage, and unyielding faith. You are an "Entrepreneurial Giant," poised to leave an indelible mark on your industry and the world.

Now, my fellow entrepreneur, the baton is yours. Carry forth the victorious lessons you've learned, the enabling insights you've gained, and the spirit of unwavering faith. As you continue your journey, remember that your breakthroughs are boundless, and your legacy is in the making. Onward, to conquer and to thrive!

Biblical Examples of Entrepreneurs

Joseph (Genesis 37-50): Joseph's ability to interpret dreams led him from being a slave to becoming the second-in-command in Egypt, where he managed the country's resources during a famine.

Lydia (Acts 16:14-15): Lydia, a dealer in purple cloth, demonstrated adaptability and hospitality. She embraced Paul's message and opened her home to him and his companions.

Dorcas (Acts 9:36-42): Also known as Tabitha, Dorcas was a seamstress who used her skills to create garments for the needy, showing compassion and entrepreneurship.

Bezalel and Oholiab (Exodus 31:1-11): These skilled artisans were appointed by God to craft the furnishings and items for the Tabernacle in the wilderness.

Nehemiah (Nehemiah 2:1-8): Nehemiah combined his leadership skills with entrepreneurship as he oversaw the rebuilding of Jerusalem's walls, addressing challenges and inspiring others.

Ruth (Book of Ruth): Ruth's commitment to her mother-in-law, Naomi, led her to work in the fields, gleaning grain to provide for their needs.

Boaz (Book of Ruth): Boaz, a landowner, demonstrated kindness to Ruth by allowing her to glean in his fields, showcasing a blend of business and compassion.

Aquilla and Priscilla (Acts 18:1-3): This couple were tentmakers who hosted and supported the Apostle Paul during his journeys, combining their business with ministry.

Zacchaeus (Luke 19:1-10): Zacchaeus, a tax collector, underwent a transformation when he encountered Jesus, demonstrating the potential for ethical business practices.

Gideon (Judges 6-8): Gideon's resourcefulness and courage led him to defeat the Midianites and deliver Israel, showing strategic thinking and leadership.

Abraham (Genesis 12-25, 13:1-3): Established a prosperous household and managed resources such as livestock, silver, and gold.

Job (Book of Job): A very industrious farmer. Managed vast resources, suffered losses, and later regained prosperity.

Solomon (1 Kings 3-11): Engaged in trade, building projects, and wisdom-based governance.

David (1 Samuel 16-2 Samuel 24): Shepherd, warrior, and king with strategic prowess.

Noah (Genesis 6-9): Built the ark and managed resources for survival.

Elijah (1 Kings 17-19): Prophet who relied on God's provision during drought.

Joshua (Book of Joshua): Led the Israelites into the Promised Land, exhibiting leadership.

Paul (Acts and Epistles): Used his skills in tentmaking alongside his ministry.

Jabez (1 Chronicles 4:9-10): Prayed for blessings and expanded his territory.

Elisha (1 Kings 19-2 Kings 13): Successful farmer. Prophet who performed miracles and advised leaders.

Amos (Book of Amos): Shepherd and farmer called to prophesy to Israel.

Rahab (Joshua 2, 6): Used her home for business and protected Joshua's spies.

Jael (Judges 4-5): Strategically used her skills to defeat an enemy general.

Isaac (Genesis 26:12-16): Farmer who was great at what he did.

Jacob (Genesis 30: 31-43): Creative livestock manager.

Apostle Peter (Matthew 4:18): Commercial fisherman.

Apostle Paul (Acts 18:3): Tentmaking business.

Esther (Book of Esther): Used her influence as queen to save her people.

Daniel (Daniel 1-6): Served in government roles and maintained integrity.

Barnabas (Acts 4-15): Encouraged fellow believers and worked alongside Paul.

Simon the Tanner (Acts 9:36-43): Provided lodging for Peter and others in his house.

Ananias (Acts 9:10-19): Played a role in Saul's conversion and ministry.

Nabal (1 Samuel 25): Wealthy landowner known for his harshness and refusal to help David.

Hagar (Genesis 16): Sarai's maidservant who became an entrepreneur after bearing Abraham's child.

Jesus (Matthew 14:13-21) (Mark 6:30-44) (Luke 9:10-17), and (John 6:1-15): While the Bible doesn't explicitly depict Jesus as an entrepreneur in the modern sense, there are instances where his teachings and actions demonstrate qualities akin to entrepreneurship. The story of feeding the five thousand is an example. Jesus saw a need, an opportunity to serve, and he turned to his disciples to find a solution. Just like an entrepreneur identifies a problem and seeks to address it with innovative solutions, Jesus looked at the hungry crowd and recognized an opportunity to meet their needs in a remarkable way.

31 Affirmations for the Entrepreneurial Giant

Here are 31 affirmations inspired by the book "Entrepreneurial Giants: Drawing Strength from Biblical Principles for Business Breakthroughs" that you, as an everyday entrepreneur, can say, repeat, and meditate on to empower your journey.

1. I am an Entrepreneurial Giant, drawing strength from timeless biblical principles.
2. I harness the wisdom of scriptures to fuel my business breakthroughs.
3. Every challenge is an opportunity for growth and innovation in my journey.
4. I embrace the power of faith, knowing that with God, all things are possible.
5. My actions are aligned with biblical values, creating a legacy of integrity.
6. I am resilient, standing strong like a giant against the storms of entrepreneurship.
7. Through perseverance, I conquer obstacles and rise to new heights.
8. I am a vessel of creativity, using biblical inspiration to innovate and lead.
9. My business decisions are guided by divine wisdom, ensuring success.
10. I am fearlessly forging new paths, empowered by biblical courage.
11. With each setback, I transform into a stronger, more determined entrepreneur.

12. Inspired by biblical heroes, I navigate the trenches with grace and determination.
13. In times of uncertainty, I rely on biblical principles to find clarity and direction.
14. I embrace challenges as opportunities to showcase my Entrepreneurial Giant spirit.
15. Every day, I embody the entrepreneurial legacy of strength and resilience.
16. With God's guidance, I build bridges of connection and collaboration.
17. I am not limited by circumstances; I draw on biblical principles for breakthroughs.
18. Through faith, I turn setbacks into stepping stones towards my business success.
19. I am an Entrepreneurial Giant, manifesting abundance through biblical principles.
20. My journey is illuminated by the timeless wisdom of biblical stories.
21. Like David facing Goliath, I conquer challenges with unwavering faith.
22. My actions reflect my values, creating a lasting impact on my business and community.
23. With biblical perseverance, I persist until I achieve my entrepreneurial dreams.
24. I am a beacon of hope, using biblical principles to inspire those around me.
25. I am a catalyst for change, transforming obstacles into opportunities.
26. I am fearlessly stepping into the unknown, empowered by my Entrepreneurial Giant spirit.
27. Through biblical wisdom, I make strategic decisions that lead to breakthroughs.

28. Each day, I channel the strength of biblical heroes as I navigate my path.
29. My business is a canvas for manifesting greatness through biblical principles.
30. I embrace challenges as stepping stones to my entrepreneurial destiny.
31. With the spirit of an Entrepreneurial Giant, I walk in faith, strength, and purpose.

Repeat these affirmations daily and let them empower, encourage, motivate, and uplift you as you navigate the entrepreneurial trenches with the guidance of biblical principles.

About the Author

*"God doesn't **CALL** us because of our education, knowledge, wisdom, readiness, or preparedness, but He **CHOOSES** us based on His understanding of our unique abilities and potential."*

–Dr. Roy L. Johnson, Jr.

Dr. Roy L. Johnson, Jr., a beacon of unwavering determination and heartfelt commitment, stands as a living testament to the power of a purpose-driven life. Born and raised in the heart of Houston, Texas, Dr. Johnson's journey was sculpted by dreams that knew no bounds, and a resolute spirit that refused to yield to adversity.

Dr. Johnson's journey began with audacious goals that would eventually see him become the first in his family to done the cap and gown of a college graduate. Armed with a biology degree from Texas A&M University – College Station in 2004, Dr. Johnson's thirst for knowledge remained insatiable. He fervently pursued higher education, obtaining an Master of Business Administration with a

Healthcare Management focus, a Master's degree with a Project Management specialization and most recently, his Doctor of Philosophy degree in Christian Leadership and Business. The pursuit of excellence became his guiding star.

But Dr. Johnson's passion for learning didn't stop at formal degrees. He embarked on a journey to equip himself with a diverse array of skills, gaining certifications as a Professional Life Coach, Entrepreneurship Coach, Life Purpose Coach, and more. Through every challenge and uncertainty that crossed his path, Dr. Johnson embraced them as opportunities for growth, soaring through tempests with the grace of an eagle, breaking barriers, and dispelling limitations.

Embracing his destiny as a trailblazer and firestarter, Dr. Johnson's entrepreneurial spirit found its home. "The Launchologist" emerged, the force behind The Business Launcher LLC, igniting dreams and nurturing aspirations into tangible realities. Through his infectious optimism, he feverishly and altruistically empowers others to navigate from stagnation to manifestation, breathing life into their visions, and nurturing the seeds of ambition.

Dr. Johnson's influence extends beyond words, gracing the platforms of The Voyage Houston, The Voyage Austin, and other prestigious publications. His impactful voice resonated in Puerto Vallarta, Mexico, as a motivational speaker, spreading inspiration that spans borders.

As one of the authors of "Strategic Entrepreneurship, The NIA Way," Dr. Johnson's wisdom is etched into pages that empower others to conquer challenges with resilience and dedication.

Not one to rest on laurels, his journey continues to break new grounds. Crowned Mr. MIBOP 2022 and Mr. MBLEP 2023, Dr. Johnson's regal spirit is matched only by his humility. He graced the cover of Queendom Magazine, shattering stereotypes and proving that dreams know no boundaries.

His legacy soared higher still, as he now holds the position of Admissions Growth Specialist of Strategic Growth Leaders Bible University (SGLU), received the esteemed Educator of the Year Award from Entrepreneur Empire Awards, and inclusion in the 2023 Marquis Who's Who, an accolade that etches his name into history.

With grace and humility, Dr. Roy L. Johnson, Jr. clearly understands and values the significance of paying forward the blessings he's received. His life story is an authentic testament to the boundless potential of education, an inspiration for both the young and the wise.

As the soil of transformation is tilled by champions unyielding, Dr. Roy L. Johnson, Jr. stands tall, a beacon of hope, strength, determination, uncompromisable faith and a guiding light to a future defined by dreams realized and lives transformed.

Explore his offerings and bask in his wisdom, for Dr. Johnson's journey is a tapestry of dedication, resilience, and an unwavering commitment to a world where every aspiration finds its wings.

To book Dr. Roy L. Johnson, Jr. for your next event or hear about upcoming events, courses, and more please visit:

www.entrepreneurialgiants.com

References

Please be advised all scriptures were obtained from:

(n.d.). No Title. Bible Gateway. Retrieved June 5, 2023 - September 15, 2023, from https://www.biblegateway.com/versions/New-King-James-Version-NKJV-Bible/

www.ingramcontent.com/pod-product-compliance
Lightning Source LLC
Chambersburg PA
CBHW060529130626
46553CB00002B/695